The Care and Feeding of Friends

Books by Ilka Chase

THE CARE AND FEEDING OF FRIENDS

WORLDS APART

THE SOUNDS OF HOME

AROUND THE WORLD AND OTHER PLACES

THE VARIED AIRS OF SPRING

FRESH FROM THE LAUNDRY

SECOND SPRING AND TWO POTATOES

ELEPHANTS ARRIVE AT HALF-PAST FIVE

THE CARTHAGINIAN ROSE

THREE MEN ON THE LEFT HAND

THE ISLAND PLAYERS

ALWAYS IN VOGUE (*with Edna Woolman Chase*)

NEW YORK 22

FREE ADMISSION

I LOVE MISS TILLI BEAN

IN BED WE CRY

PAST IMPERFECT

The Care and Feeding of Friends
by Ilka Chase

1973
Doubleday & Company, Inc.
Garden City, New York

ISBN: 0-385-01595-X
Library of Congress Catalog Card Number 72-97270
Copyright © 1973 by Ilka Chase Brown
All Rights Reserved
Printed in the United States of America
First Edition

To Spice, the cat, who walked on the typewriter keys, riffled the pages of the manuscript, tested the recipes—who, in short, helped write it, this book is dedicated.

It is also dedicated to all those friends who so generously gave of their time and yielded up their culinary secrets and without whom it obviously could not have been written. To them my gratitude and my affection.

CONTENTS

The Care and Feeding of Friends

CHAPTER ONE

Friendship and Entertaining

Once having secured the essentials for survival—the air itself, not easily come by these days—shelter, food and, for most of mankind, clothing, with such time and energy as may be left us we are supposed to get on with the quest for higher things. Enriching life for our fellows and, hopefully, enjoying it ourselves.

The framework in which this dual aim may be pursued is spacious, ranging from locations where people have virtually everything to where they have nearly nothing. But everyone, rich and poor alike, has what he considers an irreducible minimum which he must possess if life is to hold any savor.

Notions of what is irreducible are as varied as the individuals who hold them and some people's minimums appear to others quite maximal. Yet ignoring the comparative the minimum, I think, does exist. It may be a person, a job, a way of life—whatever it is it causes us to say and quite often to mean, "Without it I'd as soon be dead." I am not speaking of the high plateaus, of the sonorous themes: Give me liberty or give me death. God or Mammon. I would rather die on my feet than live on my knees. It's a far far better thing I do than I have ever done.

These are the great ethical symphonies and a chilly little bunch

1

they are, emphasizing death as they mostly seem to do but there are light operas too, popular music so to speak, that add zest to living and are important to individuals.

Your bourgeois Frenchman, for example, fancies a good little farm with a good little wife and a good little wine from his own little vineyard. To many, scarcely an irreducible minimum. *Au contraire.* The good life and not so little.

Others say, "I can do without a lot but I must have the sky beyond my window." Or a cottage small by a waterfall. Noisy and damp, I should think, but another's dream.

Most Americans would go into catatonic shock without baseball. A fourth for bridge and many a desperate trio is salvaged. Were all libraries to suffer the fiery fate of that of Alexandria, scholars would languish and perish. Others will settle for the daily paper, but it is essential. There are many of these grace notes that, could we be assured of them, would greatly enhance the quality of life. No rain on weekends, for instance. Lovely hair and long eyelashes for the girls. Attractive single men for dinner parties. And for that matter more men than women, so that women who want men in their lives would stand a likely chance of getting them.

The soufflé that never falls. And money. Not wealth beyond the dreams of avarice—although it might be fun to take a whack at that, just for the hell of it—but enough money left over after taxes to educate the kids and still travel and entertain one's friends.

These last two, travel and entertaining, though perhaps a little lush to be classified as irreducible minimums, are the privileges that I myself most cherish. Advantages without which my life would be greatly diminished.

My husband and I have traveled enough for me to have filled seven books with our journeys and we hope very much to continue enjoyable and fascinating ventures; but when not junketing about the world, when at home, I am passionately at home and then, for me, happiness is friends to dine and friends for weekends in the country.

The reason for the latter, I think, is because our life is such that we must spend much of our time in town and the country is for fun and holidays. Many people feel that way yet even so care must be taken. Eager as one may be for their companionship one is ill advised to try to seduce with bucolic charms those who are ill at ease in the country.

Invite rather the chums who fit into the background like figures in a painting. Like Monsieur Manet's "Déjeuner Sur l'Herbe," for example. Although the ladies are not required to take off their clothes. Indeed with today's see-through and mini fashions, requirement is unnecessary.

Sometimes however we have to face the fact that certain people plain don't fit. Then we must firmly remind ourselves that simply because they do not spark to dogwood and azaleas, to roses and a quiet beach, to cardinals and pheasants and dahlias and garden fresh corn does not mean they are uncivilized. To my way of thinking they are missing much that makes life worth while, but then, I can't stand baseball and from the expression on the faces of some of my fan friends when I say so I know they are thinking "Poor, poor soul, what can we do about her?"

However, despite the fact that I do not care to watch or to listen to baseball—I don't care for prize fights either—I have a warm spot in my heart for both those endeavors. Indeed for any sport in which people compete with people. They have one incomparable virtue. No animal is being hurt by them.

If two men wish to pummel each other to death, that is their business. They stepped into the ring voluntarily.

No bull enters the ring voluntarily. No cocks voluntarily attach spurs to their feet and enter the pit of their own accord. No fox summons the hounds to hunt it to exhaustion and tear it to pieces. These charming pursuits are thought up by humans. Let them demolish each other if they must or win trophies in the sports world, but leave the beasts alone.

Of course when one has sportive friends who not only enjoy the country but are willing to lend a hand with the unending chores that are a concomitant of country living one has hit the jackpot.

3

And this is where the family comes co-operatively into play. The co-operation may not always be eager but a shrewd combination of cajolement and haranguing usually does the trick in getting them to participate in the less glamorous but necessary tasks. Other wiles failing, a little set of thumbscrews comes in handy. With very junior recalcitrants the classic threat, "Well, well, Santa Claus is certainly going to be sorry to hear about this" may be invoked with gratifying effectiveness.

And I have noticed the pride that invariably follows an unaccustomed achievement and suffuses the achiever with a warm glow.

"I must say, the terrace does look a lot better now that I've weeded between the flagstones," or "My raking that driveway sure makes a big difference." Happy reward for both householder and noble guest.

Yet unquestionably there are adjustments to be made if one wants to cement and prolong a friendship. There are, for example, people toward whom I have very tender sentiments but they simply do not care for animals. Dogs and cats bore them and wild animals they find offensive.

While we do not incarcerate our pets when these eccentrics are visiting us neither do we star them and under *no* circumstances do we take them with us when visiting those who do not warm to them. And even I, a devotee of beasts, can manage nicely without endless conversation about a beloved animal.

I remember as a child that my mother had a friend named Eloise and Eloise had a dog named Mikey Boy who never left her thoughts or her chatter, and although Mother too was fond of animals, we were as one in our wish that Mikey Boy might be gathered to that Long Avenue of Trees Way Up Yonder, and preferably the day before yesterday.

Like everyone else, my husband and I prefer pets who are housebroken. Carpets and upholstered furniture come high and a chill must inevitably pervade the air if a visiting cat sharpens his claws on the back of a sofa or when dear little Fifi messes on the brand-new living-room rug.

Yet, distressing as that performance may be, with very young pups the potential for damage is not too great if caught immediately. We have found that if a wet spot is detected almost as the culprit skips off or slinks away and is blotted up and doused liberally with white vinegar and then, if handy, soda water which, after a minute or two, is gently mopped, the aftereffect will be almost nil. An application of one of the anti-dog stains currently on the market also helps.

Obviously it is still better if the desecration doesn't occur. Less strain on the entente between host and guest.

Indeed this kind of thing can cause a crisis. I once knew a widower who refused to receive his married daughter because whenever she came to stay with him she insisted on bringing with her her African Hornbill, a bird who relieved himself all over the house, making a mess almost impossible to clean up. I liked my friend, but my sympathies lay with her father when she exclaimed plaintively, tears in her large brown eyes, "Daddy let a little thing like bird shit come between us."

As far as dogs outdoors are concerned I await with interest the result of the periodic flaps over their relieving themselves in city streets. Nobody says it's attractive, but all living creatures defecate, and I would rather have to watch where I am stepping, always hoping that city dogs are curb-trained, than to see dogs forbidden to city dwellers. Nor am I much impressed by cries of "People before animals. Think of our children! of the diseases they may contract!" Nonsense. Who with any intelligence lets a child play in the gutter in the first place?

Yes, I too know about ghettos and broken homes and straying children and they are tragic but they are not the fault of dogs. Were the human race to exercise a little common sense and birth control such grim circumstances would be greatly reduced.

I have been in cities where there were almost no dogs at all or at least none visible to the naked eye. Reykjavik for one, Leningrad and Moscow for two, and to me there was something missing, something was radically awry.

Still, I am aware that emotions on the subject vary and are

5

both strong and hair-triggered and when even blood ties are strained by issues of the sort, not to mention by the profounder differences of politics and religion, it is a warning that we should be doubly alert in the selection and treatment of our friends.

Friendship to a great extent must be based on equality of affection, of compatibility, mutual interest, and trust. This doesn't mean that there won't occasionally be violent disagreements but unlike lovers, when friends recognize each other's tender areas they will not, as a rule, impinge upon them with the deliberate intent to hurt. Rather will they tactfully skirt those issues that are likely to spark fireworks.

Also, if friends have had a fairly all-out row, even though they will usually part amicably with comments such as, "Never mind, I love you just the same and thanks for a grand evening," it is prudent to call up soon afterward and return the hospitality. If we want to hold on to them let us heal the breach, even though we consider Johnnie and Connie crackers on certain issues.

Nor is there any use in pretending that in some fields competition does not color friendship. I am not a joiner by nature. Women's clubs, exclusively female enterprises, are not my cup of tea, but that may be, to a great extent, because I am a working woman. Writing, acting, lecturing, trying to run two houses with limited help, do not leave me much time for the girls. When they are engaged in definitely worthwhile enterprises, that is my loss.

Yet I have observed that ladies may profess friendliness toward one another on, let us say, charity committees and in women's clubs across the land but the competition, the jealousy over who is chairman, who deserves credit for the flower arrangements, who sits next to the speaker of the day is keen.

The friction between women competing with women is bad enough. When it is wives defending their husbands' positions the infighting is lethal. What can happen among doctors' wives on a hospital committee where everything is supposed to be very top-lofty because of suffering humanity is hair-raising. I don't know why, but the wives of doctors seem to be more *accented* than those of other men. When they are nice women they can be very special indeed but one gets the impression that some doctors pluck their helpmeets from broomsticks as they swoosh by in the darkness of Walpurgis night.

This being the case among ministering angels, what goes on among the females on army posts or naval stations with rank rampant I prefer not to think.

In fairness, however, it is not only the ladies who embrace their friends with a dagger in the hand behind the friend's back. Among gentlemen struggling to maintain and improve their foothold in a competitive world, the behavior of so-called friends can be both comical and horrifying.

Nevertheless, despite intramural battles, like squabbling families professions will usually close ranks against outsiders. This is certainly true of the entertainment world where a little bunch of thespians may be at dagger points with one another but will still present a disdainful façade to outsiders, civilians as they are thought of, who come prying out of curiosity, seeking the lowdown on what such and such a star is *really* like. And happily, when professional friendships are genuine they are the most abiding of all.

Yet in every field, professional and non-, it is, I think, a common experience to have friends by whom we are courted, others whom we court. Within reason.

If we know people we are fond of without false pride we should be willing to make the effort to keep them within our orbit. But again common sense and a sense of proportion must guide us. One or two negative responses to an invitation may be based on genuine inability to accept due to any number of causes. However, if, after a decent interval, one tries again and is refused, if the invitee never calls back then I am afraid, incredible as it may seem, we must accept the fact that that person or couple simply doesn't cotton to us. Well! Their loss, and good riddance to bad rubbish. We're not *that* crazy about them anyhow. All very comforting. We are still stuck with the unpalatable truth. We've been turned down.

7

And in a way unrequited friendship may be more wounding than unrequited love. Even when we agonize over the realization that the one we are in love with does not love us in return we say to ourselves, with bitterness or rue or a kind of black humor, depending on our temperaments, "Well, if the chemistry or sex or whatever the *hell* it is isn't working, if it isn't there, that is the fault of neither. It is a sorry heartbreaking fact and no one is to blame." And we get drunk or make a stab at suicide or, chin up, press on regardless.

But to be denied the balm of friendship—"Where have I gone wrong?" we ask ourselves. "What is there about me that they don't like? Am I so dull, so unsympathetic that I cannot attract those I care about?"

Somewhere along the road it happens to us all. Let us try not to be too downcast.

But then too there are the mystery types. They always accept your invitation and apparently have a high old time in your company. Do they ever ask you back? They do not.

"Why is that, Granny?"

"I don't know, my child. They say there are born guests and born hosts and it may be true."

And of course there are other reasons not all that inscrutable. There is work involved in entertaining and there is expense. These days, with soaring prices, food is a major item in the budget yet to some extent expense is a peripheral excuse. No one asks you to serve caviar or squab or roast beef or cherries a $1.79 a pound. Perversely, the costly cuts are the easiest prepared. You pop a roast into the oven and it does its own work with no more than a passing glance from you or a squirt with the basting tube. You serve a delicious boeuf bourguignon or lamb stew whose cost is not astronomical, everybody gobbles it up but you work like twenty Trojans preparing it. There are occasions when one must choose between time and money.

A friend of mine, Mrs. Reginald Rose, my dear Bertha, was once giving a buffet luncheon for twenty members of a garden club. She had planned two or three cold dishes and a hot fish chowder.

This last had been made the day before but imperfectly refrigerated overnight, and when she tasted it shortly before the ladies were to arrive she discovered to her horror that it had gone bad.

A woman able to cope with a crisis, our Mrs. R. opened cans of cream of chicken, cream of mushroom, and cream of celery soup. She mixed them together, adding as much milk as she had soup, pinches of spices such as oregano and thyme, a little Beau Monde seasoning, and a generous dollop of sherry. She then summoned to her aid a troop of cooked and shelled crabs, shrimps, and lobsters, heated everything together, sprinkled finely chopped parsley over all and served it up with éclat. The garden-club ladies went into transports over the delicious homemade chowder.

When on the first of the following month the gratified hostess got the fishmonger's bill, spots danced before her eyes and she had an acute dizzy spell, but she had saved the day. A pyrrhic victory, perhaps, but one she cherished nonetheless.

When Bertha told me the story I thought her triumph sounded so good I asked her a few specific details; what to do if one wanted to serve the gorgeous stuff but say to a measly eight or ten instead of twenty. Mrs. Rose went into conference with her indispensable Margaret and with a slight assist from Mr. Kahler, the fish man, came up with the following.

Mrs. Rose's Fish Chowder

(Serves 8–10)

1 can condensed cream of chicken soup	3 soup cans milk
	Pinch of thyme
1 can condensed cream of mushroom soup	Pinch of oregano
	¼ cup sherry
1 can condensed cream of celery soup	1 pound cooked shellfish

In large saucepan, mix the soups together. Add the milk and seasonings; heat through. Add the sherry and sea food; heat through. One kind of sea food is adequate. Three are living!

9

Delicious it is. Cheap it isn't, but we all have our bursts of splendor.

Money, money, money. Where *doesn't* it raise its ubiquitous little head?

While mutual interests and tastes, similar backgrounds, common experience such as work, travel, warfare, all tend to bring people together, there is no point in blinking the fact that the arms enfolding friends frequently seem to be shaped like financial brackets.

If we are to take as a simile the established Tens—Ten Richest, Ten Best-Dressed, Ten Best Plays—then, just as those entries may be at the top, middle or bottom of the list, so with friends. They may be differently placed in their particular decade but in their social contacts they are not likely to move too far above or below it.

Fortunately, within those somewhat flexible limits, incomes overshadowing our own have little influence on a genuine relationship. When affection is involved friends want to be together and money doesn't count.

Even so. No matter how appreciative we may be of the good times they provide, no matter how desirous of holding up our end, frequently we are shy about asking richer chums to come to us. This may also be the case with celebrities even if money is not involved.

It just so happens that we know that famous TV character quite well and while he may be the soul of hospitality, it's scarcely likely, or so we feel, that his Tiffany personality will be seen to its best effect in our humble setting.

But here again one must be guided by the individual and the closeness of the relationship. Some Croesuses or limelight figures are perfectly capable of making their own beds and stacking the dishwasher. Others are pained by the housekeeper's prosaic tasks or are frankly inefficient.

It is also human if those who work hard all week offer a silent prayer that the house where they are to spend the weekend will boast enough service for them to be able to relax.

Such niceties of temperament are what the hostess must be able to detect. We might also add that a civilized reaction to the situation in which he finds himself is the guest's obligation. But even if one must occasionally tread delicately, for many people, among the happy experiences of life, receiving friends ranks high.

CHAPTER TWO

The Single Woman Entertains

If a woman lives alone, oddly enough giving a dinner may prove more involved than having friends as house guests, while in turn an outright party can be simpler than one or two for dinner.

The reasons for this are the Balanced Table Syndrome and the Wary Male.

Regardless of finances, a lone lady giving a dinner seeks first a beau, an escort, an opposite number for herself. Then, since the chances are she is inviting another single woman, unmarried, divorced, or widowed, she takes pride in matching her up too. Married couples fall into place easily enough.

If our lady is young and pretty, unattached males are not likely to prove much of a problem. If she's all *that* young and pretty she won't have trouble attracting a straying married man either. But let's say she's in the middle years: not girlish but by no means old. She will have her difficulties and the reason is obvious. Attractive men of her own age are, by now, married. And if they aren't they care nothing at all for a woman of suitable years. They hunt more tender game. This, with a few blessed exceptions, means that the available men are homosexuals. There is a great deal to be said for them.

13

To begin with they are people. My opinion of the human race is not high but I belong to it and I recognize members of the club when I see them.

Homosexuality in either sex is perhaps one of nature's more humane ways of defending herself against gross overpopulation and would seem preferable to mass destruction by war, flood, famine and disease.

It does seem to me unfortunate that followers of the cult should have elected to call themselves gay. Gay in its original sense was a delightful word. Blithe, happy, sprightly, lighthearted . . . all its connotations were charming. This is no longer the case. I still use it because it pleases me but I am aware of the shadowy echo.

Obviously, a homosexual is not the dream of a female who wants either a husband or a lover, but from the point of view of a woman of any age, the thing to remember about a dinner is that people are invited to eat, drink and entertain one another, not to breed.

Many homosexuals are extremely pleasant companions. They are intelligent, they have taste, they are usually informed about and interested in the arts. Indeed many outstanding artists have been and are of their persuasion. Perhaps not so many as they claim but a tidy number. Frequently they themselves are experienced hosts and helpful to the hostess.

They can be demons for work and, as has been proven time and again, in wars they are often outstandingly courageous. The mixed blessing aspect of homosexuals is that as a rule they have mates. This can be a bonus if you need two extra men and a nuisance if you want only one, since they are as firmly cemented together as the most devoted heterosexual couple.

Either way, society being what it is, they are a fertile field for the entertaining single woman. To deny it or to evade the issue is fruitless. I remember Chessy Patchevitch, one of New York's most charming and celebrated hostesses, telling me of a friend, a widow of position, wealth, and advanced years also well known for her hospitality, who announced in stentorian tones, "I will *not* have pansies at my dinner table."

"In that case, dear," Chessy said dryly, "you're in for some damned lonely evenings."

We come now to the other facet of the single woman's evening entertainment problem, the Wary Male. Let us say she is a professional woman or, let us say, she is not. She has some money and a job is not a necessity. Either way she can fill her days satisfactorily. Come evenings she would like a little companionship. Sometimes, however, she has neither the time, strength or inclination to go in for a full-scale dinner yet she doesn't want to be lonely.

One man for dinner would be ideal or at most a man and a couple. Most single women hesitate to ask a couple to dine with them in a restaurant knowing that the husband will either feel embarrassed having her openly pay for his food—the fact that she pays for the home-cooked meal is a veiled expense—or he will simply not permit her to do so and her invitation is down the drain. If, fortunately, she belongs to a club, any embarrassment is automatically eliminated. She is the member and nobody else *can* pay.

If she wishes to entertain in a restaurant, probably the most graceful way to go about it is for her simply to sign the check, having arranged beforehand for the head waiter to take care of the tips. If it is a restaurant where she is well known she may not even have to sign. The bill will be sent to her or put on a credit card.

Then too she may hesitate to ask a couple to come to her house if she is alone, feeling that if it's going to be that intimate and informal they would doubtless prefer to be at home.

Asking a man, a heterosexual man, if by herself is even more complicated. He is wary prey and, no matter how pleasant and offhand the ambiance, leery of being hooked.

If the lady herself merely wants an evening's companionship, maybe followed by a bit of hurly-burly, well and good, but if deep in her heart she wants marriage she must be a skillful angler to keep her trout from sensing that fact.

How the idea that the thought of marriage must originate exclusively with the male and break upon the woman as a glorious surprise ever got so firmly established in American society is mysterious. That the surprise element is pure fable goes without saying.

I specify American society because, although the pattern is changing in Europe, for generations marriage there was arranged by the parents, the two young principals having little voice in the matter.

The system had and has many disadvantages but a virtue is probably the very fact that since it is largely a business matter the fiancés can be perfectly candid in their reactions to one another.

And in any event, regardless of which side of the ocean you're on, why should a woman's very normal desire for a man of her own and a home of her own and children be treated as though it were some shameful secret?

Now that Women's Lib is daily gaining ground, the point of view probably seems laughably old-fashioned, and a good thing too.

For a great many women, however, even when marriage and finances are not involved, male companionship is preferable to solitude or to a night out with a group of the girls.

How to achieve it? As frequently happens, the light touch may be the best way to go about it. Supposing our lady has met a man who catches her fancy at a dinner party.

A couple of days later she might call him up and say, "Hello, this is Jemima Jenson Jones. We met the other night at the Twaddle Twitchets, remember?" You can bet he'll remember the name, if nothing else.

"Why, Miss Jenson Jones, of course. How are you?"

"Very well, thank you. And you know, I'm indebted to you. I was *fascinated* by what you were saying about the balance of trade credits between Japan and Nigeria. It's the kind of thing that interests me *very much* and I'd like to learn more about it. I wonder if you have a free evening if you'd come to dine with me? I have a good cook (or, I'm not a bad cook if I say so myself), and it would be such a pleasure to see you. Perhaps I can get the Twaddle Twitchets too."

"That's very kind of you. Why yes. How about next Tuesday?"

"Perfect. Shall we say seven-thirty?"

"Righto."

The deed is done. The single lady needn't be too serious about the Twaddle Twitchets although when her guest arrives (and try to think of him as a guest not a victim), she might say with engaging candor something along the lines of "Actually I didn't try the Twaddle Twitchets, but I did want to get hold of the Guston Goostons. I know you and he would get on. He's keen on bilateral agreements. There's nothing he doesn't know about Afghanistan-Solomon Island International Trade Negotiations. Unfortunately he had to leave for Kabul this afternoon."

Who knows but what this wily yet innocent play that started out as a simple sociable evening may not lead eventually to the altar? Of course if it does the lady may live to rue the day she ever told that little white lie about her passion for international trade agreements. She'll be fed to the teeth and up to the ears for life.

Even in this emancipated age, I believe, statistics prove that the vast majority of women marry, hopefully, for love, but certainly for support. Theoretically the great hunter still brings home the bacon. And I have yet to hear of a female wage earner who would not be charmed, not to be relieved of the necessity to work if she is enjoying her job, but to have the family income supplemented by a gainfully employed male.

And when children are involved, even with the rash of illegitimacy which has infected us, Dad's hand on the tiller is still considered by many mothers to be a sound idea. If, by some happy fluke, Mummy and Daddy are married and love each other, the kids are in clover.

Incidentally the following is a menu Jemina Jensen Jones might consider serving to her lucky prey.

Artichoke bottoms with chopped ham
and béchamel sauce
Scaloppini of veal with tarragon
Small boiled new potatoes
Asparagus with melted butter
French chocolate mousse
With the meal a pleasantly dry white wine.
da Gaucette 1970 is a nice one
Black coffee, Italian or French roast, afterward.

Now, about those artichokes. You can of course use canned, but there's no question that fresh are better. I know, it kills me too to discard all those leaves, but you don't have to. You can save them and cook them the next day, but the delicious bottoms, the prize, you obviously will not have to look forward to, since it will already have gone on safari through your alimentary canal.

If however you want a dinner to be extra special, be ruthless. Remove all the leaves. For the deed you will require:

Artichoke Bottoms with Chopped Ham

(Serves 2)

2 artichokes	Madeira
Juice of 1 lemon	⅓ cup finely minced boiled
1 tablespoon flour	ham

Remove the leaves and chokes. Trim the bottoms with a sharp knife and rub them with lemon juice. Cook in lightly salted boiling water to which you should add a little lemon juice and flour. In Paris this is known as a fond blanc. Cook until tender, about half an hour, remove from water, and drain.

Place in a small dish, cover with Madeira, and let stand for about an hour. Remove, pat dry, and fill the bottoms with the finely minced boiled ham. Cover with béchamel sauce.

Béchamel Sauce

(1 cup)

3 tablespoons butter	Salt and pepper to taste
2 tablespoons potato or arrowroot flour (in a pinch you can use regular flour, but the others are more delicate)	1 small onion
	2 whole cloves
	Pinch freshly grated nutmeg
	1 bay leaf
1 cup milk, scalded	Pinch of thyme
1 chicken bouillon cube (optional)	Few sprigs parsley

Make a roux, that basic combination of butter, flour, and milk. Melt the butter over low heat. Add flour gradually, blending well without browning. Stir in milk (if desired, add the chicken bouillon cube to the milk, stirring until dissolved), stirring constantly. Continue to cook and stir until smooth. Simmer for another 5 minutes, and continue to stir, over low heat, to avoid an uncooked flour flavor. Season to taste with salt and pepper. Add the onion, studded with the cloves, the nutmeg, bay leaf, thyme, and parsley, these last tied together for easy removal.

If you have plenty of time, you can stir and cook over a low flame for 25 to 30 minutes, but a labor-saving device is to put it in a 350° F. oven for about 20 minutes.

The beauty of this dish is that it can be prepared in advance. Even the sauce, if you dot it with butter. Everything may be kept at room temperature for an hour before serving. When ready to serve, place the minced ham on the artichoke bottoms, reheat the sauce, stirring well, and pour it over them. A sprinkling of paprika and finely chopped parsley gays things up a bit.

Scaloppini of Veal with Tarragon

(Serves 2)

1 pound veal cutlets, thinly
   sliced
¼ cup flour
Salt and pepper to taste
¼ cup butter
1 tablespoon lemon juice
2 tablespoons chopped fresh
   tarragon *or*

2 teaspoons dried tarragon,
   crushed
½ cup dry white wine or
   Madeira
½ cup beef bouillon

Most butchers will slice the scallops very thin, but you yourself may want to put them between sheets of wax paper and pound them even thinner. To be sure they will be especially tender, soak them in milk for several hours before cooking.

Season the flour with salt and pepper and dredge the veal lightly. Melt the butter in a frying pan, and when it foams, pop in the scaloppini. Add the lemon juice and tarragon. Cook the veal for 3 minutes on each side.

Remove veal to a heated platter and deglaze the pan with the white wine and beef bouillon. Simmer briskly for a minute or two; pour over the meat and serve hot.

The following dessert is appropriated from that great treasury of culinary art *The Joy of Cooking*. There are countless recipes for Chocolate Mousse but this one is delicious and may be got out of the way well in advance of the dinner hour.

French Chocolate Mousse

(Serves 2–3)

1 cup milk
2 tablespoons sugar
1½ ounces grated sweet
   chocolate

2 egg yolks, beaten
½ cup heavy cream
½ teaspoon vanilla
1 tablespoon brandy

Stir and scald in a saucepan over low heat the milk, sugar, and grated chocolate. Pour these ingredients over the beaten egg yolks. Return the sauce to the pan. Stir the custard constantly over low heat until it thickens. Strain. Cool by placing the pan in cold water.

In a separate bowl, whip the heavy cream until stiff. Add the vanilla and brandy. Fold the cold custard into the whipped-cream mixture until it is well blended. Pour the chocolate into custard cups or little chocolate pots. Chill thoroughly before serving.

If you can't get fresh asparagus, you might consider substituting braised endive. Also try subtly to inform yourself of your man's stand on desserts. Most men like them, and the richer the better. Some types however turn out to be surprisingly spiritual. They can't *bear* sweets. They prefer a simple fruit dessert or what they *really* dig is cheese and crackers. In this event get bona fide *good* cheese, *not* pre-sliced rubber sheets with paper in between. If you want to put on the dog and there are only two of you, serve with it a half bottle of red wine. White wine would be preferable with the rest of this particular meal but it doesn't complement most cheese as well as red does, a well-known exception being cheese fondue made with imported Swiss cheese and white wine.

Apropos of desserts in general: if the rest of the meal has been hearty, a formal dessert course may seem a bit too much, or possibly you are rushing off someplace after dinner and want to hurry things along a bit. In that case a pleasant period to the meal may be delicious cookies or perhaps special candies served with coffee.

Braised Endive

(Serves 2)

2 or 3 Belgian endives per person, depending on size
Boiling water
1 tablespoon lemon juice

¾ cup chicken stock or bouillon
Butter
Beef extract *or* Bovril

Preheat oven to 350° F. Remove any imperfect outer leaves and blanch the endives briefly by dipping them in a sieve into the boiling water. Drain them and pat dry.

Arrange side by side on a well-buttered shallow flameproof baking dish. Combine the lemon juice and chicken broth; pour over endive in dish. Dot with butter. Cover and bring to a boil on the top of the stove; boil for about 10 minutes. Uncover, and continue boiling until the liquid is reduced.

Place buttered brown paper, wax paper, or cooking parchment over the endives; cover with a lid. Place in oven and bake 1 hour. Remove the lid, but not the paper, and bake 25 minutes longer. Sprinkle with a few drops of the meat flavor and bake 5 minutes longer.

Serve hot in the dish in which they have been cooked. The advantage of asparagus or endive is that with these vegetables you don't need a salad. With anything starchy, such as peas or Lima beans, you might want one.

CHAPTER THREE

The Single Man Entertains?

No, the question mark after the above four words is not a typo-
graphical error. It is a query both skeptical and startled because,
let's face it, how many times does a single man repay his social
obligations? Very, very rarely.

In a sense this is the fault of both hostess and guest. The hostess knows she's lucky to get an attractive unattached man at her
dinner table. Even if he is relatively modest he knows the same
and he knows that she knows it. It's a question of supply and demand. She's in short supply, he's in great demand, he's bound to
be asked back anyway, so why bother?

That this is a cynical attitude is obvious, but it prevails today
and probably always has. One cannot of course issue a blanket
indictment. Often a man will send flowers or bring a book or a
record, perhaps a couple of bottles of wine or liquor to his hostess,
and very pleasant it is.

I even know one or two delightful men who will ask a married
hostess, if her husband is not keen on the theatre, to go to a play
with them and take her to supper afterward. Such gestures, however, are rare. Even when single men have the wherewithal, sometimes they just don't like spending it.

I am reminded of a friend of my mother's who used to beau her around when I was a child and after she and my father were divorced. He was a nice man and I was an avid reader, so he cannily brought me books enlisting my support in his campaign as a wooer of my ma.

I think Mother liked him quite a lot, but nothing much came of it and one reason was that he used to amuse her but possibly in the wrong way.

I remember her telling me that when they went out for an evening almost invariably he would turn to her at the end of dinner, or at the box office if they were buying theatre tickets and say, "Miss Edna"—he was a formal beau—"Miss Edna, I happen to find myself a trifle short. I wonder if you would be good enough to advance me a little money. I shall return it tomorrow."

Once Mother caught onto this ploy she came prepared and as she said, "He *was* scrupulous about returning the money. Always there was a check in the next day's mail. I think it was the cash itself he couldn't bear to part with."

Younger men of course frequently are short of cash, and if they are agreeable companions who bring amusement and interest to a dinner table, a hostess is already grateful and properly so. They have helped her to make her house a magnetic rendezvous for those she is fond of and enjoys seeing.

But as a rule older men of relatively sophisticated circles have *some* money in their jeans. How about parting with a little of it in return for several free meals and weekends?

Even single men have to have a roof over their heads. They have even been known to have cooks and cleaning women, or, in the old days, the affluent bachelor's trademark, the Filipino boy. And, as they are the first to tell you, the best cooks are men. Well then? What is so difficult about asking you and a couple of other pals to spend an occasional evening under their roofs sharing the host-cooked yummies?

They might even go so far as to suggest a restaurant, but let's not attempt to run before we can walk. Tiny steps for tiny feet.

24

First a small group in for drinks in the late afternoon perhaps. Then, at a later date, a little home-cooked dinner might be forthcoming, and *then*, oh but a *long* time after that, if the market has done its stuff, a modest binge on the town. Merely a thought tossed out at random for the single chap to mull over.

And of course there is a category that should not be forgotten. The bird hunter whose own lair is a little apartment equipped with soft lights, the hi-fi, a *very* well-stocked bar and a bed that would cause Don Juan and Casanova to exchange looks of sheer incredulity.

In such a milieu the chance for adventure is great, the chance of being served nourishing victuals slender.

But even if at a stage in his life where, as a result of disillusionment, exhaustion, or a newly developed sense of prudence, the hunter is not on the prowl, one reason, I think, that the indisputably male, unattached man isn't more generous with his social hospitality is because frequently he is divorced or in the throes thereof and the little woman has taken him to the cleaners. If she is marching in the legion of Women's Liberation she has also quite possibly said, "O.K., Buster, these three kids are yours too, *you* look after them for a change." And the fruit of his loins is dumped right back in his lap.

Conditions such as these are valid alibis yet it is not unheard of that a lack of reciprocal social behavior is a matter of laziness as much as economy.

If you work all day, giving a dinner party is a chore when you have to cope with it yourself.

That I have never known a professional working woman to use that as an excuse for not convening her friends is, I suppose, to be ascribed to the female's nesting instinct.

I know several single women who work—in stores, schools, offices, or at home writing or painting, and I have yet to see one of them who couldn't cope—willingly and very often without any outside help at all—with an occasional festive evening.

A great general may be a whiz at logistics, but disregarding genius, I think the average woman is a better organizer than the average man. She plans ahead. This is probably why women are so much in demand as secretaries. "My dear," says the boss, "you have an uncanny knack for details." The truth is, were he willing to concentrate, even an average man could probably be pretty uncanny too, but details are frequently boring. It is a whole lot more fun in an office to execute the all-over grand design in a free-wheeling, slapdash manner, and if a woman is being *paid* for the detail she doesn't have much right to beef. It's when the "uncanny knack" routine is practiced in the home by the husband that little Madam occasionally feels irked.

Interestingly enough, homosexuals, possibly because of a certain femininity inherent in their natures, are far more likely to be good and reciprocal hosts than the truck-driver-football-executive types.

They like preparing the party, they enjoy the party, and they are good about cleaning up afterward. In your house or theirs. Also, since many of them are in the decorating business, the locale of their own festivities is likely to be attractive. On occasion bizarre but usually attractive.

And in fairness it must be said that if the single male's hospitable instincts are dormant through the winter—he's a great hibernator—comes the summer solstice, things perk up considerably.

We all number among our friends the barbecue brigadier, the guru of the grill. Mention to these fellows the Fourth of July or a beach picnic under the stars and *stand back!* They're off at a gallop. Comical aprons, chef's caps, sacks of charcoal briquettes, asbestos gloves, cases of beer . . . the props materialize and multiply as at a magic show.

Sometimes more enthusiasm than skill is brought to bear, but who cares? It's great fun seeing them have fun and if the meal really does turn out, it is a triumph.

Needless to say, such virtuosi are rarely single and the reason is obvious. A woman has only to see one and he arouses the instant Diana in her nature. A toot on her hunting horn and she's off to bag him. He's a prize, he's a treasure, he's her own true love and a hell of a cook to boot.

I once complimented a friend of ours on the buffet luncheon her husband had prepared singlehanded. She gazed at him fondly. "Well dear, he's good in the hay and he's good at the stove. What more can a woman ask?" In that particular instance the husband was also good in the office, and the money rolled in. *That* lady's irreducible minimum was nicely taken care of. And by way of the plop of the cherry on the top of so faultless a structure the husband enjoyed his work. All of it.

And therein, I suspect, lies the secret of happy entertaining as well as happy life in general. Male or female or a sprinkling of both; married, single or going together, have a good time and you'll have a good party. There are just two things to remember. While we not only can and hopefully will do without the blood, sweat, and tears we can rarely do without the toil. The other thing is that next to our own happiness and that of our children there are few things so rewarding as seeing people we are fond of enjoying themselves and knowing that we have helped to make that enjoyment possible.

A good menu for a single man to tackle—and you don't have to be a single man to do it—might be a steak or casserole, a tossed green salad, French bread and cheese, a nice wine, and for dessert either fruit or a good boughten ice cream. Little sweat, much pleasure.

A succulent recipe for a casserole, by the way, I owe to Eleanor Howard who first devoured it in New Mexico—I myself have devoured it in *her* house, and, looking into the pot afterward, it occurred to me she'd barely have to wash it. Cleaned out!

Bean Pot New Mexico

(Serves 4–6)

2 cans (approximately 1 pound)
   kidney beans
¼ cup sweet pickle juice
2 tablespoons vinegar
2 tablespoons bacon fat
2 cloves garlic, crushed
2 whole cloves
1 bay leaf
¼ teaspoon thyme

¼ teaspoon rosemary
Salt and pepper
2 onions, sliced
6 slices bacon, cooked and
   crumbled
¼ cup black coffee
3 tablespoons (1½ ounces)
   whiskey

Preheat oven to 350° F. In a 1½-quart casserole, combine the kidney beans, pickle juice, vinegar, bacon fat, and seasonings. Bake ½ hour. Top with the sliced onion, and crumbled bacon; bake 20 minutes longer. Remove from oven. Add black coffee and whiskey—and serve.

More audacious types might want to branch out, to break new ground.

A bachelor friend of ours, Walter Goodman, enjoys entertaining friends in his charming house overlooking the water. To be his guest is a pleasant experience, but one is wise to wear dark glasses when visiting him.

The reason is he breeds Skye terriers. He breeds the best Skye terriers in the country—some say in the world—and they have won every blue ribbon and every silver cup and every silver bowl in every dog show in the U.S.A. In 1969 one of them, Champion Glamoor Good News, known around the house as Suzy, went Best in Show at Westminster. Walter, his family, his pals, were delighted. The only thing is that with all that silver on display when you enter Walter's house you are blinded by the glare of sterling.

Mr. Goodman and his friends have even won twelve silver mint julep mugs, and while you are sipping he is whipping. He is whipping up an especially good quiche Lorraine and this is how he does it.

Quiche Lorraine Gautier

(Serves 6–8)

1 9-inch frozen pie shell	1 cup (4 ounces) grated
8 medium-thick slices bacon	imported Swiss cheese
3 eggs	¼ cup grated Parmesan cheese
2 cups heavy cream (or half	¼ cup grated Cheddar cheese
milk and half cream)	Nutmeg
Salt and pepper to taste	Butter

Walter Goodman unabashedly takes the short cut of prepared pie crust.

Follow directions on package for baking pastry shell. Leave in its own plate.

Preheat oven to 375° F. Cut the slices of bacon into small strips and simmer for 5 minutes in boiling water. Rinse in cold water, dry on paper. Brown lightly in a skillet. Place drained bacon pieces on bottom of baked pastry shell.

Beat the eggs, cream (or cream and milk), and seasonings in a mixing bowl until well blended. Combine the grated cheeses; add to the egg mixture. Pour into the pie shell. Sprinkle with nutmeg and dot with butter.

Set in upper third of oven and bake 25 to 30 minutes or until the quiche is puffed and browned. It may then be slid out of its pie plate onto a decorative plate for serving.

This recipe prepared up to the point of putting it in the oven to bake also freezes very well.

CHAPTER FOUR

How About a Little Dinner Party?

You may go for quite a time without doing any entertaining and then one morning you wake up and you feel it coming on. A kind of pleasant influenza creeping over you. You realize it's been a long spell since you've seen Evvie and Mary and Nancy, dear funny George and Alex and the Harpers and the Griggs. How about it?

"How about it, honey?" you say to your husband, who, while not anti-social, could go a good eight months impervious to the fact that you haven't had a human soul in the house.

"How about what?" he asks.

"Giving a little dinner party. It's been quite a spell since we've seen . . ." and you run down the list.

"Great. Fine. Why not? Anything you say."

American husbands are *so* obliging. "All right, but is there anybody special you'd like to ask?"

"Anybody you want is O.K. with me."

"Any particular kind of food you'd like to have?"

"No. Whatever you plan will be fine." Obliging but not exactly co-operative. Still it's a lot better than "For God's sake, don't tell me we're having people here again?" or an even more anguished

"We're not going out again *tonight,* are we?" Well, they get tired.

If you sit at home alone all day writing you get tired too, but you have been alone and in the evening you crave a little sociability.

In an office you've been seeing people all day and if you're a doctor you've been seeing the ill, the dying, and the hypochondriacs, and by nightfall you may be forgiven if you feel you've *had* the human race. Still, the chances are that if they are at your dinner table the guests will be in pretty good shape and they'll cheer the man up. And by the time the evening of the party arrives, he's usually feeling that way too.

It occurs to me though that sociably inclined American wives might occasionally pause for reflection. Many American husbands die early. The number of widows in the United States is a melancholy statistic.

I remember once holding forth on this topic to Eleanor Howard. Eleanor is the wife of Mr. Jack Howard of the Scripps-Howard newspapers and television stations. They are a merry, gregarious, entertaining and frequently entertained couple.

Commenting on the sudden and shocking death of a mutual friend, Eleanor said, "Jack says he's coming to the same end if we don't stop all this partying. We've been out every night for two weeks and we're going to be out Friday, Saturday, and Sunday too."

"Listen, Eleanor," I said sharply, "you can't do that to men, they've got to have some letup. They aren't as durable as we are, you have to realize that."

"Oh," said my friend. It was, for her, a very small Oh.

There was a slight pause.

"Of course," I added, "I suppose I shouldn't talk. Norton and I have been busy the last four nights, and we're tied up for the weekend too."

Eleanor burst out laughing. "My God," she said, "you scared me to death. For a minute I thought you meant what you said."

Well, I do. I chose my moment inauspiciously, yet I do not think

32

men should be subjected to an accelerated pace for too long a stretch.

But to return to partying. Within reason. In Great Houses, I daresay, entertaining doesn't present too much of a problem. The mistress simply summons the chef, announces that there will be ten for dinner, Thursday evening the fifteenth and will he please concoct three or four alternate menus, one of which she will select.

I'm not envious. I even get a certain kick in thinking there are people who live that way. I don't wish them carted off in tumbrils or, as in England, taxed to the point where they have to open up the historic hall and charge admission in order to keep the slates on the roof and the drains unclogged. It's simply that I don't know any of those people and our way is not their way.

In our house if Thursday the fifteenth is good for Norton, considering his appointments that day and the next, I call the waitress we usually have to ask if she is free that evening and can come to help out before I dream of calling any friends.

If a couple or a single person is doing the dinner themselves, they of course plot the service as expeditiously as possible, and guests help as much as they can or as they are allowed to.

Otherwise the number of extra help is largely dependent not only on finances but upon the temperament and abilities of one's Staple, the live-in maid.

We once had Kathleen, and a pearl and a gem she was, but if we tried getting in extra help the explosion could be heard for miles around.

I feel it is not too demanding to expect a cook-housekeeper, with help from her employer, especially in setting the table and perhaps cooking or buying one dish, to cook and serve a dinner for four or even six, if it is informal and simple. More than that and aid is usually called for. For eight, one waitress, if the maid can leave the kitchen and help her to serve. If it is a formal dinner with dishes that need last-minute attention two waitresses are preferable as otherwise the service is very slow. For ten, two are virtually a must. A buffet is something else again.

I appreciate that anyone under thirty who may read this book is not likely to have the foggiest notion of what I am talking about yet I persist. Many young people are historically minded. They may regard these tracings as the record of a quaint and long passed era, yet even today, when such amenities *can* be managed they contribute to a pleasant way of life.

Also, although not too many people do it, I find that reminder cards are not a bad idea, especially if an invitation has been issued considerably in advance of the party date.

On occasion, with the best intentions in the world and every desire to attend the festivities one may forget. And it has been my experience that when that happens nine times out of ten the forgetters were not engaged in any superior glamorous activities but morosely dining alone.

If we are giving a party naturally I consult the linchpin of our household, Elisabeth. Occasionally, for reasons I cannot help, it may be that we would like to have the dinner on what is usually her day off. Since Elisabeth is a dear about changing, I dislike taking advantage of her and ask her indulgence only if I am in a jam; a place I try not to get since I do enough housework myself to know that it is an occupation from which one needs frequent divorces.

Our "staff" having been alerted, I then start calling up the chums. Any hostess knows that what she may undertake as a lighthearted gambit can be fraught with frustrations. Few things are more discouraging than to ask those to whom you are devoted, only to have them say, "Sweetie, we'd love to come. Thanks so much, but we're going to be in Hong Kong on the fifteenth."

Once in a great while the shoe is on the other foot, and although I genuinely regret having to decline an invitation from someone I like, I imagine the lilt in my voice is audible when I say, "Sweetie, I'd love to come, but we're going to be in Africa." Since we have been in Africa five times I have on occasion detected a slight note of acidity when my would-be hostess asks, "When *aren't* you going to be in Africa, dear?" Mostly we are not in Africa, but I know the feeling.

34

But let us say that everything has come up roses and we have actually been able to gather together what we feel will be a congenial group. We then turn to the menu. I have found, incidentally, that matters usually go more smoothly if one's treasure, a good maid, has her day off after the party rather than before. The reason is twofold. A, after the ball she is probably tired and needs the rest and B, a great many dishes are much better if prepared the day before.

Obviously not a steak, unless you are serving cold steak which, properly done and accompanied by a mustard sauce can be delicious, but almost all stews and casseroles profit from an overnight marriage. The same is true of cooked fruits and of a certain orange dessert. If served the second or even third day their flavor is greatly enhanced. Here's how you do them.

Baked Fruit

(Serves 4–6)

1 can (1 pound, 13 ounces) cling peach halves	1 tablespoon lemon juice
	¼ cup light rum
1 can (1 pound, 14 ounces) unpeeled apricot halves	Grated rind of 1 orange
	1 tablespoon grated lemon rind
1 can (1 pound) Bing cherries	¼ cup blanched almonds
Syrup from canned fruits (about 3 cups)	1 tablespoon butter
	Heavy cream
Juice of 1 orange	

Preheat oven to 325° F. Butter a shallow 2-quart baking dish (the oblong Pyrex ones are good). Drain the syrup from the peaches and apricots and combine with about half the syrup from the cherries. Arrange the peaches hollow side up in the dish. Arrange the apricot halves between the peaches and dot with about 18 to 20 pitted cherries. You don't need too many, but they add flavor and color. The fruit should completely cover the bottom of the dish. Pour about half the syrup over it to just barely cover the fruit.

Place in the oven and bake for 2½ hours. The only trick to this is that you do have to watch it, as the syrup reduces gradually, and more must be added. Check about every 20 minutes. First add the orange and lemon juices, then remaining fruit syrup as needed.

Sprinkle with grated orange rind, lemon rind, and rum. Sauté the almonds in butter; sprinkle over fruit and continue baking ½ hour longer. The fruit will darken, but it mustn't blacken and burn. The finished result should be fruit in a thick syrup rather than juice. Serve in the baking dish and pass heavy cream to go with it.

This is a delicious but rich dessert most appreciated if the meal preceding it has been relatively light and without thick sauces. It may be served either at room temperature or cold.

Now for the orange dessert.

Orange Compote

(Serves 6)

6 navel oranges
Boiling water
1 cup granulated sugar
1 cup (12-ounce jar) red
   currant jelly

Juice of 1 lemon (optional)
¼ to ⅓ cup water

Remove the outer skin of the oranges with a vegetable peeler so that it is very thin. Cut in narrow strips, julienne style. Cook in the boiling water to cover for 30 minutes, changing the water twice to eliminate the bitter taste of the peel.

Cut away all white membrane that remains on the oranges; cut into slices crossways.

In a deep saucepan, combine the sugar, jelly, lemon juice (the lemon juice is optional, but I use it since I do not care for excessive sweetness), and water; boil for 10 minutes. Add the cooked peel to the syrup and boil 15 minutes longer.

Put the orange slices in a bowl; cover with the syrup mixture. When cool, refrigerate to chill. Serve cold. Your favorite kind of cookie is a pleasant accompaniment. If you prefer cake it should be something like pound cake, as the syrup itself is quite rich and thickens slightly with the passage of time.

The advantage of the above kinds of food, the stews we mentioned and the fruit recipes, is that come the party the hard work is behind you and whoever does the cooking, employer or maid, feels a great deal freer.

Speaking of advance preparations, every hostess has her own set pieces which may be her pets but which nevertheless she is willing to undertake only two or three times a year. My own candidate for one of these is boeuf à la mode en gelée. Great food, but brace yourself. It takes a good three days to prepare. Well actually, a night and two days. The overnight marinating, the cooking and cooling the next day and the application of the aspic the day you are going to eat it. These are time-consuming processes but the reward is great.

All recipes exhort you to turn your beast every two or three hours, and while I can hardly imagine anyone setting an alarm and getting up for the purpose in the dead of night, if you *do* happen to be awake, paddle out to the kitchen and give it a whirl. It's all in a good cause. If you are serving this glorified pot roast hot you can polish it off in a night and a day: the twelve-hour or more marination and then getting it to the stove so it will be done by dinner time.

| BOEUF À LA MODE | HOT POT ROAST |
| BOEUF À LA MODE EN GELÉE | COLD POT ROAST IN ASPIC |

The left side titles look grander than the right, don't they? Ah those French! Never mind. By any name it tastes the same. Every cookbook you pick up has a slightly different version of this great old classic and, like most people, I have snipped a bit here and a bit there to effect this concoction of which there is rarely any left over. Rump of beef is the best cut, although others can serve. But whatever you choose, beware! It diminishes somewhat during the cooking and you can get a nasty shock when you take it out of the pot. That little smidgen? What ever became of the great, gorgeous thing you put in there?

Boeuf à la Mode

(Serves 8 to 10)

Allow about ½ pound of beef per person. Should there be any left over, don't worry. It's marvelous the second or third day too. With only one or two very small variations, the following is from *Mastering the Art of French Cooking*, which in my opinion is the best of the several recipes I have experimented with.

4 pound rump of beef
5 or 6 strips of larding pork if the needle is to be inserted by loving hands at home
1 cup each: finely sliced carrots, onions, and celery stalks
2 unpeeled cloves of garlic, cut in half
2 bay leaves
½ cup minced parsley
Pinch of thyme
Pinch of oregano
Salt and pepper
5 cups dry red or white wine. Some people prefer white, but in our house we follow the Communist line

½ cup olive oil
½ cup brandy
4 or 5 tablespoons tried-out beef or pork fat *or* cooking oil
1 split veal knuckle
1 split calf's foot if it is obtainable. Usually it isn't.
4 to 6 cups canned beef broth *or* homemade beef stock, in the unlikely event you should have any
1 tablespoon arrowroot, cornstarch, or potato flour
2 tablespoons Madeira or port

Your chunk of beef should be larded with four or five ribbons of fresh pork. Most butchers will do this for you, but a tasty trick is to soak the strips in brandy for an hour or so. If you have a larding needle at home and are a couturière, you can insert the fat yourself, going with the grain of the meat. Otherwise, take a tot of brandy to your butcher and pray that he is an honest man

38

who will neither tipple nor toss it away as a nuisance, assuring you he has done the job you requested.

For marinating purposes use a procelain, enamel, or Pyrex bowl just large enough to hold the meat, vegetables, and liquids.

Make a shallow bed of the sliced vegetables, herbs, salt and pepper in the bottom of the bowl. Place the larded meat on top. Pour in the wine, olive oil, and brandy and cover with the remaining vegetables and herbs. Cover the bowl. Marinate at least 6 hours (12 to 24 hours if the meat is refrigerated). Turn and baste every few hours while you're awake.

The next day, about half an hour before you plan to start cooking, remove the beef from the marinade; place on rack to drain. Dry more by blotting with paper toweling.

Preheat oven to 350° F. Using a Dutch oven or flame-proof casserole, heat the bacon fat or cooking oil; add the beef and brown well on all sides. This is tedious and takes time (20 to 30 minutes), but it is a must. Remove meat and drain off the fat.

Pour in the marinade and over high heat reduce it by half. Then add the veal knuckle and calf's foot and enough broth to cover about ⅔ of the beef. Cover and bring to a boil. Immediately reduce heat and skim off as much fat as possible. Place casserole in oven and cook so that the liquid remains at a gentle simmer. Turn meat occasionally and allow about three to three and a half hours. Test by piercing with a fork. If it is done, the fork goes in easily.

Remove the meat and keep hot. An electric platter and the meat covered with foil is a good system, or you can put it on a dish and replace it in the oven with the heat turned off.

Skim the fat off the cooking liquid and strain through a sieve lined with damp cheesecloth. Return liquid to pan and cook over high heat to reduce it quickly to about 3½ cups. If the sauce seems thin, thicken it with the arrowroot, cornstarch, or potato flour which has been mixed with the 2 tablespoons wine. Season to taste.

Carrots and onions are the classical accompaniment to pot roast. They may be braised separately, or, if the pot is big enough, added to the meat the last half hour of cooking. In this event, be sure to lift them out with a slotted spoon and keep them warm with the meat while you make the gravy.

When ready to serve, pour some of the gravy over the meat and pass the rest separately. Noodles or mashed potatoes go well with this hearty dish and the delicious sauce.

Boeuf à la Mode en Gelée

(Serves 8–10)

If planning to serve the beef in aspic, proceed as above until you have strained the cooking liquid and reduced it to 3½ cups. Soften 2 envelopes unflavored gelatin in brown stock or canned consommé; add to the hot liquid and stir over low heat until the gelatin is dissolved. Remove from heat; add ¼ cup brandy and strain. Slice the meat and arrange with a thin layer of cooked carrots and onions between the slices in a rectangular mold or baking dish deep enough to hold the sliced meat and vegetables. Pour in the gelatin mixture. Refrigerate 4 to 6 hours or until well set.

To turn out onto a cold platter insert the dish momentarily in hot water, run a knife around the edge between the meat and the dish. Put the platter on top of it and reverse. Serve surrounded by watercress.

In summer if you are offering your boeuf à la mode in aspic I think you might forgo the potatoes and serve a tossed green salad. Hot French bread with or without garlic butter is compatible. A pretty and delicious dessert is half a watermelon filled with its own meat formed into balls combined with berries and other fruit such as strawberries, blueberries, white grapes, cantaloupe balls, and fresh, pitted cherries, the whole well sprinkled with kirsch or rum. If grape leaves are available, line the melon shell with them before so they will stick up over the rim of the shell before putting in the fruit. Décor. Caramel custard is another dessert thought, and if it's a rainy summer Sunday and you feel the need of one hot dish, clear hot tomato madrilene to start with might fill the bill.

The aforementioned orange compote would also be a good dessert with this particular meal and combined with the next two dishes makes a successful luncheon.

Serve as an entree a string bean and Lima bean casserole. Follow this with roast chicken and green salad and then the compote.

String Bean and Lima Bean Casserole

(Serves 4)

1 package (10 ounces) frozen Lima beans *or* 1½ pounds fresh Lima beans	4 tablespoons butter
1 package (10 ounces) frozen green beans *or* ½ pound fresh green beans	3 tablespoons flour 1½ cups milk, warmed ½ cup chicken broth Salt and pepper to taste Freshly grated Parmesan cheese

Cook the frozen beans separately as directed on package; drain and keep warm. Cook fresh Lima beans in small amount of boiling water for 20 to 25 minutes; drain and keep warm. Do the same with the string beans.

Meanwhile, in a saucepan, melt butter over low heat. Add flour gradually, blending well without browning. Add the warm milk and chicken broth, stirring constantly. Continue to cook and stir until smooth. Simmer another 5 minutes, and continue to stir, over low heat, to avoid an uncooked flour flavor. Season to taste with salt and pepper.

Place the cooked beans in a shallow 1-quart casserole; cover with sauce. Top with generous sprinkling of Parmesan cheese. Place under broiler to brown. Serve at once.

This dish may be served with the meat, but it is so good it deserves star billing.

All right. Now let us say that the menu, whatever we have decided on, is under control. As the hour of the party draws near it is to be hoped we are all such good housekeepers that there doesn't have to be any extra spit and polish, the place is *always* ready for inspection. Even so, most of us give an extra quick flick of the dust cloth. I know only three women for whom this does not hold. They and their houses are superbly organized 365 days a year. One is Mrs. James Ziegler of whom more anon, another is Mrs. Frederick Trapnell. Mrs. Trapnell lives in California and is married to a retired admiral and the term shipshape was invented for the admiral's wife.

I was speaking to the third not long ago. I'll tell you who it was too. Dorothy Rodgers, Mrs. Richard Rodgers, the wife of the composer.

"I'm a wreck," I said. "I've been trying to clean out the accumulation of twenty years from seventeen closets and a filing cabinet."

Because she is a friend, Mrs. Rodgers clucked sympathetically but her glance was vague, and having been in three of her houses I know quite well that an accumulation of twenty years is something that simply does not happen there. Mrs. Rodgers keeps abreast of herself.

Well, I try to keep things reasonably clean and tidy. Intense disorder I find fatiguing, but as anyone who lives in a New York apartment knows cleanliness is not easy. Frankly that's one reason why it's better to entertain at night. The grime doesn't show so much.

If the windows haven't been washed for a while you draw the curtains. The soft and pretty fabric immediately forms an attractive background. As long as the furniture is dusted and polished people are not likely to notice that the walls could do with a coat of paint.

Even when we ourselves are aware that the place is a bit shabby it is the atmosphere we create that counts, rather than the details. At least that's what I firmly tell myself.

As far as extra party preparations are concerned, many can be done in advance. Do you perhaps have sconces on either side of the fireplace? Candles on the table? Take care of the new ones the day before. There's a chore that's a real nuisance. Cutting open those cellophane wrappings, then either shaving down the candles if they're too fat or wrapping extra bits around the ends if they are too slender to stand firmly in the holders.

These days, now that so many people no longer smoke, I always have to make a note to myself to buy cigarettes. It makes me happy to offer our friends the best we can but I confess to a mingy streak when it comes to cigarettes. Norton is a great pipe and cigar man. I occasionally join him in the latter indulgence but neither of us goes for cigarettes and I never know what kind to buy. It was simpler in the old days when, if people were determined to give themselves lung cancer, they acquired it through Lucky Strikes, Camels, or Chesterfields.

The minute the party is over I rush around gathering up whatever is left in the cigarette boxes, wrap them in Baggies, and put them in the fridge till the next hoe-down. Sometimes of course I forget and then on checking their boxes I am disconcerted to find all those dried-out, stale-looking, and I don't doubt stale-tasting, little paper tubes. In any event I fear our offerings are on the lean side, as I have noticed that many people come to our house supplied with their own brands, but they do anticipate ash trays and matches and these we try to supply. Although at that you might make a note to stock decorative matches. Those handed out by the local supermarket don't exactly fit into the gracious living scheme.

If wine is being bought especially for a party, it is better to lay it in a week to ten days beforehand.

I was speaking to young Mr. Michael Aarons, scion of the noted house of Sherry-Lehmann, about this and he said plaintively, "Miss Chase, you have no idea how many people will order really expensive wines from us the day they plan to drink them and then call up muttering and grumbling, saying how disillusioned they are, that the wine wasn't at *all* what they expected. Of course it wasn't. The sediment didn't have time to settle."

The settling is less important for white wine than it is for red but ordering well in advance is a good rule for both. Also, according to Mr. Aarons, the younger the wine the longer time you should open the bottle before dinner allowing it to "breathe." With a wine such as Beaujolais you don't have to worry too much. It's better when it isn't over two years old in any event, and it is such an accommodating charmer that you can open it and drink it right away.

The other ahead of time note refers to flowers. By and large they are best bought the day of the party although occasionally for tightly furled beauties—gladioli for example—you may want to have them in your house a day or even two days before so that the blooms will have opened. If you and your florist are on good terms, let him know your wants a little ahead of time.

In New York we deal with the East River Florist, the setting for the well-known Katie. Katie is German, comfortably upholstered, and the shop is a joy to visit. Not only because the flowers and plants are fresh and varied but also because little birds, little finches fly about free. Two small brownish-red umbrellas hanging upside down from the ceiling serve as their private quarters but they have the run or fly of the store and they perch on the large and strong plants and flit among the flowers, chirping merrily. They must be content because every once in a while a new member is added to the community.

Katie advises and helps me select the merchandise she feels will best serve my purpose and she told me that if you have short-stemmed flowers which, for some reason or other, you must get the day before the party you can assist survival by placing them in a vase in water and setting it in the refrigerator overnight. Almost all florists advocate the use of the white powders, Flora-life, Bloomlife—there are several—for helping to prolong freshness. With blooms that tend naturally to longevity, such as asters and marigolds, it is surprising how long they will last. Easily ten days to two weeks.

When I have powder in the vases I usually content myself with adding a little fresh water daily. If I do not have it, I change the water completely and snip the stems a trifle. With some flowers—dahlias, poinsettia, snow-on-the-mountain—milky stems, the tips of the stems should be singed.

44

Naturally if you have a country garden of your own you will cut what you want when you want it. But there is one thing to bear in mind. Flower fixing takes time. A little knowledge of arrangement doesn't hurt either, even though theoretically "doing the flowers" is considered to be one of the most instinctive and graceful of feminine pursuits.

In the days when drawing-room comedies flourished in the theatre, the heroine was forever drifting in from the garden, arms laden with artificial blooms which she proceeded to place into vases set strategically about the stage.

The vases obviously never held a drop of water and more than once, witnessing the business, or indeed doing it myself in my acting days, my attention has wandered from the play or from my own lines as I wondered how long the poor parched beauties were supposed to last.

While I will never win any prizes from a Japanese master of the art of flower arrangement I have adopted certain practical tricks that stand me in good stead.

Much depends on the flowers, but by and large it is better to strip the leaves from the part of the stems that will be immersed. That way the water goes up the stem to the bloom itself without being sidetracked. You may have to clip a few of the upper leaves too. The chief thing is to avoid a choked, jammed-together look unless you deliberately want to achieve a chunky, closely massed effect. Once flowers are cut they should be placed out of drafts and hot sunshine.

If you have only a few in a vase, an odd number is likely to be more graceful, less martial than, say, four or six. Mixed bouquets, the kind immortalized by the old Dutch masters, are enchanting.

The mixed bouquets of summer! They delight the eye and gladden the heart. The strong, vivid marigolds and zinnias and asters and snapdragons. Larkspur and canterbury bells, columbine and roses. I can never remember their scientific names, but I do not mind, their common names are so engaging. The pale bouquets are lovely too. I sometimes mix together white and very pale pink dahlias, lightly spiked with lavender cosmos, although my favorite cosmos is the pure white. Delicate white cosmos in a crystal vase, a summer snowfall. Varied bouquets set in baskets is one of the prettiest ways of presenting flowers.

Great spikes of gladioli create a marvelously dramatic effect, and then, as the lower blossoms begin to die off, I cut them down and in a totally different manner they are effective too. And let us not forget the naturally low beauties. Pansies and violets and nasturtiums and lilies of the valley. Nor any others. Tulips and "Daffodils that come before the swallow dares, and take the winds of March with beauty." Had Shakespeare written only that line, his name for me would still be immortal.

Every time I am involved with flowers, especially when the moment comes to discard them, I marvel at their individuality. Even those grown in the same bed, picked at the same moment, vary in beauty and longevity. Why do some last so much better than others? They are like human beings. And as I would shrink from striking down a human being so I shrink from throwing out flowers when they are still fresh, enjoying their sojourn in light and air and water. Sometimes, on leaving one house for the other, the flowers are really not sprightly enough to make transporting them worth while. I know that by the time I return they will be dead, yet I leave them in the vases anyhow. I cannot bring myself to throw them away. I do not feel as distressed when I must discard them in the country because there they are tossed on the compost heap and I know that theirs will be the resurrection and the life.

I remember I was once playing a summer engagement in Philadelphia in a theatre in the round in the park, and I was extremely unhappy. To begin with I hate having to play in broad daylight and I have always felt sympathy for the Globe company of the aforementioned Mr. Shakespeare. Also, I was not all that in love with my fellow actors and I was in a hotel to which I developed a strong antipathy the minute I set foot in it, but for assorted reasons I was obliged to stay there.

My sole comfort was reading, a strong tot of vodka at night after the performance, and two small ivy plants. No two plants were ever so pampered. They were watered, they were sheltered from drafts, they were set in the sun, they were moved to the shade if it became too strong, their soil was cultivated with a fork from room service. Those plants survived. To this day one or two of the ivies we have around the place are their descendants.

When doing the actual work of flower arranging, I spread newspapers on the pantry floor or counter onto which I clip the stems and surplus leaves. This saves sweeping them up later, as all I have to do when finished is to gather up the papers.

Whenever practical, frogs are invaluable aids for holding the stems in place and one can make pretty arrangements with fewer flowers. With small vases it doesn't matter so much, but the large heavy ones I fill only partially with water, put in only a few flowers, the upright girders so to speak, and then when I have carried them to where they belong I fill them up from a watering can and place the rest of the blooms.

Sometimes I feel quite proud of my labors, yet even then there is usually one vase that is the bastard child. The one into which you plunk the leftovers with a silent prayer that if it is noticed people will think it an original and imaginative arrangement.

Dr. Brown will often compliment me on my floral endeavors, but he has the diagnostician's sharp eye. Sometimes he will glance around the room, point silently to a particular vase, and take his leave. Who wins them all?

With flowers for the table low arrangements are usually best, as it is defeating not to be able to see a fellow guest across the way. While most of the dinner conversation will probably be addressed to left- and right-hand neighbors, the width of the table permitting, there is no law that says you can't indulge in a few exchanges with your opposite number.

A host and hostess are free to follow their own inclinations as to seating arrangements, but there is a kind of fusty old protocol that many people accept and that seems to work pretty well.

Since Norton and I do not move in exalted governmental or ecclesiastical circles we have never had the problem of who takes precedence, a Secretary of State or a bishop. I believe according to Mrs. Vanderbilt, regardless of what one may personally think, the man of God ranks higher, but even in our group we follow the convention that the oldest or most distinguished or first-time or infrequently seen guests sit at the right of the host and hostess.

However, there is a slight pitfall inherent in this scheme; it can be a little wince-making. We were dining one evening with young friends we are very fond of. It was a buffet party, and although there were a couple of quite well-known women who were also guests, I was seated at my host's right. Well now, I thought, isn't Jenny sweet. She knows how fond I am of Jonathan and has put me next to him. A little later I happened to glance around the room. I was the oldest woman there.

When coping with seating arrangements, as everyone knows, eight and multiples thereof are fraught with anguish.

Either the sir or the madam must shift places, and it's a tossup as to which member of the guest couple gets the right-hand treatment since, if the other guests are also wed, it can't fall to both of them. If they are more or less on a par, usually it's the wife, but if the husband is the Achiever, then it is he.

Too bad there should be any complications because, unless it's a very large affair, six and eight are the best numbers for a cheery evening. People can get to know each other, and as a rule they stay longer and have more fun.

As I have already said the dream of every hostess is a balanced table, failing which she will happily settle for an extra man. It's that extra woman who causes the headache. This is patently ridiculous and when this has been the case either in our house or that of a friend I have often found that the unattached lady was the star of the evening.

As far as the seating arrangements are concerned, if she is a true star she will be at the host's right. If she is a darling and an old friend she will be at the hostess' left. The idea being that there is a tiny edge of honor to the arrangement and that if anyone must be manless it is the hostess.

Things obviously will go more smoothly if details of the kind are worked out ahead of time so that the guests don't have to shuffle about, pulling chairs in and out while the hostess makes up her mind as to who goes where.

Speaking of seating arrangements, a Machiavellian joke was relayed to me by that same Mrs. Rodgers I mentioned, the neat one. She had a friend who, as many of us do, drew up a little seating plan which she put under her own plate so that when the guests went into the dining room she could quickly glance at it and allot everyone his rightful place. She then crumpled up the bit of paper and dropped it on the floor.

One of the guests, a bachelor and good friend who was often asked to the house, quietly picked it up one night when everyone had left the table.

Sure enough a few weeks later he was asked back again as were two or three of the same people who had been there before. Surreptitiously he slipped into the dining room and reaching under his hostess' plate exchanged that old seating plan for the current one. When the company went in to dinner the poor hostess drew out her little trot and nearly had a seizure. There were the names of some of the guests present all right but not of others. Was she losing her marbles? What had happened? The prankster relented and all was made clear, but Dorothy neglected to tell me just how soon it was before he was asked to return.

Ideally speaking, seating plans and everything else that is attendable should be attended to ahead of time, thus allowing oneself leeway for bathing, resting, making up, and dressing before the guests arrive.

I don't always practice what I preach but I try to keep one eye on the stars. I like to have the corks drawn from the wine bottles, the candles lighted, in winter the curtains closed and the fire crackling before the first ring of the doorbell.

Architecture permitting, nothing is so welcoming as a fire in the front hall or flowers on a table or chest. They tend to make friends feel festive the moment they come in.

A little soft background music is a mood inducer too, but if we use it I turn it off after two or three guests have arrived. People unconsciously start raising their voices to drown it out and the calculated effect perishes.

Some hostesses, when they have extra service for the party, will arrange to have the maid or butler ask the guests what they would like to drink as they take their coats.

It's a funny bit of nonsense, but nobody wants to arrive first. Why ever not? Whatever time you're invited for, *get* there. Congenital latecomers are inexcusable. It's bad for the food, plus which the hostess doesn't live who, as the minutes tick by and nobody shows up, doesn't think to herself, My God, they've all forgotten. On the other hand, I don't recommend arriving early. If, when you ring the bell, the maid comes to the door tying on her apron, the hostess is invisible, and the host emerges zipping up his fly, you may conclude that you're ahead of time.

Should this happen, however, when offered a drink don't toss it off like a Russian grand duke about to leap into his sleigh and gallop off across the frozen steppes. That betrays embarrassment. Be nonchalant. Sip. Lie. To your utter amazement a cab drew up just as you were leaving your apartment! You thought you'd have to wait at least fifteen minutes. Laugh lightly while admiring the view or the flowers.

The cocktail period before dinner varies with every household and will vary greatly depending on the temperament and number of guests. Our own span is from half to three quarters of an hour. To my way of thinking the absolute outside limit is one hour, which already strikes me as overlong.

Usually a hostess feels she must wait until all the guests are assembled, and offhand it would seem the natural and courteous thing to do. People may be late up to a point. But if as much as an hour slips by, the food can be doomed, and it is rude to expect the guests who have arrived on time to wait any longer.

We all have friends whose idiosyncrasy it is that they cannot tell time. Once having assimilated that fact for the benefit of the kitchen, one's self, and them ask them a good half hour before you ever expect to see them.

The code arrangement we have worked out with the kitchen in our house is simple. The first time dinner is announced I know I have ten to fifteen minutes' leeway before shepherding my lambs to the table. They can finish their drinks or have a dividend. The second announcement means business. Get them in as gracefully but as speedily as possible.

When Elisabeth is both officiating in the kitchen and serving at table she is a sturdy little general. She comes to the living-room door and holds up one finger. A few minutes later she reappears. If all is in order she holds up two fingers, one on each hand, but if she has reason to believe that a dish is going to be extra special she holds up two fingers of one hand, V for victory. I don't suppose it is the way they do it in Buckingham Palace, but it maketh glad my heart and the stomachs of our guests.

Some cooks are geniuses in the art of holding, or else they are well acquainted with the habits of their employers. Many years ago we knew a couple who invited us to dine from time to time. The dinner was always excellent but it was always the same. Roast beef, and the roast was always rare. What was remarkable about it was that the host, who has since died, was a man of brilliance but he was also an alcoholic. The cocktail hour went on and on and on, yet when we finally did go in for dinner there was that rosy red beast, juicy and flavorful. I sometimes suspected they bought two or three roasts and put them in the oven at twenty-minute intervals.

By and large, however, if invited for dinner I want to sit down at a reasonable hour. I want to eat and to appreciate and I want to have our own food and wine appreciated. Or at any rate tasted.

And speaking of tasting I would here like to insert a small dart into the vitals of those who will never eat anything except that which they have always eaten and who do not have the good manners at least to push the food about on their plates so that they look as though they were enjoying themselves.

I do not speak of people who have definite allergies. I know there are those who cannot tolerate shellfish, or certain kinds of nuts, one of our friends cannot eat veal, another gets the shivers if served anything that once wore feathers, and no hostess would ask her guests to contract ptomaine for courtesy's sake, but a painstakingly planned and well-cooked dinner merits a little respect.

I enjoy kidneys and calf's liver, and an occasional snail, but I am aware that many people do not. However, it's a signal dinner party where a guest is served a slice of liver. And yet, prepared as they used to do it in the great days of New York's Colony Restaurant, it can be a rare great. I admit were I confronted with rancid yak's milk in Afghanistan or sheep's eyes in Arabia it would require all my skill at dissimulation to pretend to relish them. However I am not speaking of cruel and unusual punishment and we have been in Arabia* and nothing of the sort appeared on the tables of the various houses where we were received. In any event they always have so much delicious rice one could discreetly bury an eye and the host and hostess be none the wiser.

Adri, the brilliant young clothes designer and a great friend told us that when she was in Japan ordering dress fabrics she was taken to a dinner at which ducks' feet were served. I asked her what she did about that and she gulped and said, "We had the webbing and nails and everything. Fortunately there was a sauce that made it palatable but the texture, the texture was *peculiar.*"

I have since learned that a large percentage of the ducks' feet served in the inscrutable East come from scrutable East Moriches Long Island, U.S.A.

In most houses the size of the table dictates the number of guests one will invite for a seated dinner, but there are occasions when we feel expansive. Nothing but a buffet will suffice.

* *Around the World and Other Places*

There is no reason in the world why guests shouldn't help themselves to the same kind of food and limited number of dishes they would be offered were servants passing it to them, but looking at that expanse of table, many women feel they've got to furnish it with a considerable variety.

Perhaps a sea-food casserole and rice as well as roast beef or turkey. Or maybe beef stroganoff or a superior coq au vin and cold sliced ham and a green vegetable or roast of veal and cold salmon or striped bass in aspic and a cheese board and a fruit dessert *and* chocolate pots too. The selections can go on and on in ever more delirious smorgasbord fashion, but usually three severely limiting factors control even the most imaginative and ardent hostess. Time, money and physical strength. For shenanigans of the sort just mentioned you need a plumpish balance in the bank and a staff or a caterer. Or you and your local treasure working till 2 A.M. the day of the party. Are you ready for that?

Whatever the menu may be I find card tables are preferable to laps. Balancing a plate, knife, fork, and wine glass *and* trying to eat requires the skill of a W. C. Fields at his juggling peak.

The card tables may either be set or the guests can pick up from the buffet a rolled napkin with the cutlery therein. Wine and water glasses should already be on the tables.

At a buffet many hostesses let the guests seat themselves. I do not, because I think it never works out well. The women, usually having served themselves first with the men bringing up the rear of the line, have to pick a table and either sit there alone or with other women as on an auction block, hoping to lure some man besides their husbands. If they don't succeed, the husbands feel guilty not joining the ones with whom they already eat three times a day, or, if a husband is shy, and a surprising number of them are, they seek out their wives as a port in a storm. Me, I'm not for it.

The hostess knows her guests. I feel it's up to her to concoct intriguing little combinations and set place cards so people will know where to go. When she has only one table she seats them. Why not if she has three, four, or five?

This scheme obviously is not practical when there is a real crowd: a wedding reception, a charity dance, a tennis tournament luncheon, but I find it works well for the non-spectaculars.

At some buffet parties the guests serve themselves the main course and the servants clear the plates and pass the dessert. Sometimes each person fetches his own. The system you can afford and that facilitates traffic is the one to aim for. At a buffet, coffee is usually brought to the card tables or guests help themselves from an urn. At smaller seated dinners it is often served at table too, although I myself prefer coffee and, if they are being served, liqueurs, in the living room.

It used to be that the men remained at the table and the women either went into the drawing room or the hostess' bedroom. The bedroom route is the one I follow, while Norton takes the men into the living room, the reason being that any extra servants who have come in to help can clear the table and go home at a reasonable hour. Any waitress is of course expected to clear away and wash the coffee cups and liqueur glasses, gathering them up from whatever room she has served them in.

Some hostesses, I know, feel it disrupts the sympathetic flow which, hopefully, has been established at the dinner table, if the men and women separate for coffee, and if there are only four or six people I agree that it's nonsense to break them up. Unless you're going in for experimental twosies.

With a larger number it's not a bad idea. The ladies and gents have an opportunity to take a refresher course in make-up and what have you and the girls can tell each other dirty stories while the men discuss their tailors and the stock market. Or, as in a house like ours, where doctors are often the feature players, blood and guts.

It is the hostess' responsibility however to make sure that this period is not prolonged to the point where, when the sexes are reunited, it is time to go home. This makes for a lethal evening.

Let the girls finish their coffee and whisk them back to the chaps. In the reblending, people can move about and mingle with those they haven't had an opportunity to talk with at dinner.

Should you have a piano and a guest to play it this is the golden moment to ask him to do so.

As a rule, talented people do not mind, as long as they are not urged to perform for hours on end and if they know quite well that they were invited because they are liked or loved and not merely for their skill.

If the guests are card players and if cards are the reason for the gathering, this, of course, is when the tables are set up. Bridge still being the star magnet. Although backgammon, my sophisticated friends tell me—I think of them as Regency rakes at the gaming tables—is making a strong comeback. But what ever happened to the oh so pretty Mah-jongg?

As the evening wears on many people appreciate a tall glass of soda or a highball. I feel that a waitress should pass these once but, unless it is a very formal or deluxe affair, if the guests linger she can't be expected to stay about indefinitely.

Weekend rallies sometimes continue into the wee hours but on week nights parties generally tend to break up around eleven or eleven-thirty. Certainly when the guests are working people with jobs to get to in the morning and *certainly* when they are surgeons who are kin to birds. Early to bed and early to rise and in the operating room, scrubbed, scalpel in hand at 7 A.M.

In my movie days Hollywood was considered, not without reason, to be a loony, glamorous town, but for the most part the mythical orgies were just that. Myths. When you had to be at the studio around seven o'clock and not just *be* there but looking fresh and rested for the camera, any nocturnal debauches were strictly limited.

If you entertain a fair amount a helpful trick is to keep a little book with the names of the guests and the dinner menu you offered them. That way if the Joneses play a return engagement two or three weeks later they don't have smoked salmon and coq au vin twice in a row.

I once read that the Duchess of Windsor kept track not only of the menu but also of the china, linen, and flowers used at the dinner party so as not to make the gaff of repeating the same routine

55

a second time. I was impressed but since we don't own that many sets of china and glass, I concluded that the best we could do was to make what is on the plates and in the glasses as tasty as possible.

Incidentally, speaking of dishes, I am glad that today the fashion is moribund for I never could understand the theory of and passion for matched sets. Occasionally they are still advertised by department stores but an identical pattern for everything from service plates to after-dinner coffee gets pretty monotonous. Switching with the courses makes a pleasant little diversion.

We have one friend, Harmon Duncombe, who is my lawyer and a china enthusiast. If he is intrigued by a plate he picks it up, turns it over and looks at the hallmark. I find this flattering, like people who scrutinize the label on the wine bottle. Hopefully they are not doing it so as to be sure to avoid that particular brand in future.

Besides writing the menu, I jot down notes as to whether the food was well cooked, did people go for seconds or leave a polite mess on their plates, and the wine and its vintage that was served.

I do try to plan what I hope will be delicious dinners. I am not the world's hottest hors d'oeuvre organizer. And yet I believe in them. They shouldn't take the edge off appetites, but a bit of succulent blotting paper is a good idea. I am not, however, a devotee of rabbit food. I do not salivate over raw carrots and celery, scallions and raw cauliflower flowerets and radishes cut like roses. I have noticed that many others do not either, and often the plate goes back to the kitchen untouched. It's enough to make a cook hopping mad because all that slicing and peeling and cutting takes time.

Canapés and Hors d'Oeuvre

I admit to being not all that snooty when the celery is cut into inch-long pieces and stuffed with cream and Roquefort cheese mixed with a few chopped walnuts and one raw delicacy I am definitely a fan of is offered by our friend Barbara Ziegler who is not only a knowledgeable gourmet but an inventive one. Mrs. Ziegler slices small white turnips paper thin and serves them with celery salt. Refreshing and slimming.

We ourselves serve one raw canapé or hors d'oeuvre that is simple to prepare and surprisingly popular. With a cookie cutter cut out rounds of bread (you get four to a slice), and fry them lightly on both sides in butter. On them place a very thin round of onion and on top of it a round of tomato of the same size. Sprinkle with salt and a little freshly ground pepper. That's all. If you use good ripe tomatoes they're delicious. We also make some without onion, just the tomato, for those to whom onions give a lot of back chat.

The toast rounds serve as a base for many mixtures. Hot cheese puffs or peanut butter sprinkled with crisp bacon. A little chopped chutney is often added to this or, as a change, we sometimes mix it with very finely minced crystallized ginger.

If you like pitted dates or stuffed olives wrapped in bacon I have found they are more easily achieved if you half cook the bacon first, then wrap it around whatever it's supposed to enclose, fix it with a toothpick and then finish the frying process. Water chestnuts done this way and served with a Sweet-and-Sour Sauce dip are great favorites.

These tidbits are reasonably filling so they should be small or served perhaps when dinner is going to be on the late side.

Softened cream cheese mixed with a little curry powder, rolled into balls and dipped in finely chopped chipped beef and pierced with a toothpick to facilitate serving also vanish quickly.

At the house of friends of friends we once had litchi nuts stuffed with cream cheese and finely chopped pecans—texture as well as taste was pleasing although it was a little on the sweet side.

Probably leading the festivities that rank high for Norton and me are our Christmas parties. They started some years ago when his children were youngsters. They would spend Christmas Day with their mother but come to us for Christmas Eve. Since I had a stepson from my previous marriage he joined us too, and when he in turn married he brought his wife and her family. We also asked friends we were fond of but who had no close relatives to turn to during the holidays.

Through the years the parties have become a kind of tradition. They used always to be in New York but now we have them in the country. Inevitably the faces have changed; people move away, people die or they get married and start Christmases of their own, but it is surprising how many have remained with us year after year. We count on them and we like to think they count on us.

I always want to have the tree trimmed at least three or four days before Christmas both for the pleasure of looking at it and to get the job out of the way. Children may love to help and if you have them that's the way to do it yet fundamentally tree trimming is not child's play. If you want to achieve a certain effect a lot of effort and thought goes into it.

Some fine year I shall change the scheme completely, but for the last three or four we have done the same thing. We have the tree flocked by the nursery from which we buy it in the country. They are more expert than we in achieving the snow-laden look. Norton then sets it in a metal base and sets that in a galvanized tub of water which, through the holidays, we keep replenishing. Thus refreshed the needles are co-operative about adhering to the branches. We mask the ugly tub with cotton batting.

Like everybody else, I imagine, we slip the finial star over the tip of the topmost branch and string the lights before starting with the ornaments. We use the tiny Italian bulbs and no color other than the color of the light itself.

We have many boxes of ornaments, many richly colored balls, but in recent years we have used only the sparkly ones, clear glass that looks like crystal with touches of gold, interspersed here and there with golden fruit and an occasional globe of palest,

palest pink. When the tree is lighted it has a shimmering, fairy-like quality that is quite lovely.

We have presents for everyone. They are inexpensive, but I try to find things that are appropriate to the recipient. We have discovered that at a party of this kind people enjoy having two or three small packages for the fun of opening them rather than only one present even should it be quite grand.

Our friends usually arrive bearing gifts too, which are placed around the tree with those we have already put there. We have cocktails, and the dinner is always buffet, with people seated at small tables. Our number varies between eighteen and twenty-two.

On these occasions coffee is taken at the tables. There is enough litter and confusion in the living room later on without having coffee cups in the way.

After dinner, the presents! With a big clothes basket for the wrapping paper and ribbons. Norton whips out his camera and flashbulbs and takes a few group pictures which we later distribute to the participants.

For us it is a highlight of the year but it's just as well that it does come only once. The shopping and the wrapping can take it out of you. That's another reason I enjoy traveling. In foreign lands you can pick up tidbits that make good Christmas presents without having to draw a deep breath and plunge into the maelstrom of our commercial Yuletide.

I here submit three of our Christmas menus that seem to have met with approval.

With Cocktails

Water chestnuts wrapped in bacon served with
sweet-sour sauce

Toast rounds with rounds of cucumber spread
with cream cheese and red caviar

Hot cheese puffs

Dinner

Smoked salmon. Olive oil, capers
and quartered lemons are passed
Dry white wine   with this.

Thin slices of pumpernickel bread
spread with sweet butter.

Roast venison, sauce poivrade
Red Wine   Purée of chestnuts

String beans

Endive and watercress salad

Cheese and crackers

Plum pudding with hard sauce

Pumpkin pie

Coffee

Champagne with the presents

For the venison and sauce poivrade I am indebted to Jessica
Daves. Jessica succeeded my mother as editor-in-chief of *Vogue*.
She was, at one time, a southern lady. She is still a lady, I hasten
to add, but she has been adopted by us damn Yankees for a good
many years and we claim her as our own.

Miss Daves, or Mrs. Robert Parker, coped not only with the
world of fashion but was canny in culinary fields as well. So much
so, in fact, that she, with her friend Tatiana McKenna, compiled
and wrote what I consider to be one of the best cookbooks in
my collection. It is called the *Vogue Book of Menus and Recipes*
and is a rich storehouse of ideas for food and clear and incisive
instructions on how to go about preparing it. The sauce poivrade
for venison follows.

Roast Leg of Venison with
Sauce Poivrade

(Serves 10)

6- to 7-pound leg of venison
Salt and black pepper
3 celery stalks, chopped
2 carrots, sliced thin
2 onions, sliced thin
2 shallots, chopped
3 parsley sprigs, chopped
2 garlic cloves, crushed
6 peppercorns, crushed
6 juniper berries, crushed

1 teaspoon dried rosemary
   (optional)
½ teaspoon dried thyme
1 large bay leaf, crumbled
3 cups dry white or red wine
1 cup wine vinegar
½ cup olive oil
Sauce poivrade for venison
   (see below)

Season the venison with salt and pepper. Mix the vegetables, herbs, and spices, and place half the mixture at the bottom of a deep, narrow pan. Place the venison on the mixture and spread the rest over the meat. Mix the wine, vinegar, and olive oil, and pour the liquid over all. Marinate in a cool place for two days, if possible, or at least overnight. Turn the meat several times each day so that it is well seasoned all over. Drain the meat, reserving the marinade, and dry it with paper towels. Roast the venison in a medium oven (375°) as you would beef, allowing about 12 minutes per pound for rare venison. Serve with sauce poivrade.

Sauce Poivrade for Venison

Marinade from venison
3 tablespoons olive oil
¼ cup vinegar, scant
2 tablespoons tomato paste
½ cup Madeira or tawny Port

4 cups prepared brown sauce
   (see below)
8 peppercorns, crushed
¼ cup dry white wine
2 tablespoons butter

Strain the marinade used for the venison, reserving 1 cup of the liquid. Drain the vegetables thoroughly and brown them in the olive oil. Pour off the oil and add the vinegar and ½ cup of the marinade. Reduce the mixture by simmering to one third. Add the tomato paste, the Madeira or Port, and the brown sauce. Bring to a boil, reduce the heat, and simmer for 35 minutes, stirring occasionally and skimming the surface. Add the crushed peppercorns and cook for 10 minutes longer. Strain into a clean saucepan. Add the remaining ½ cup reserved marinade liquid. Simmer for 30 minutes, skimming it carefully. Deglaze with the white wine the pan in which the venison was roasted. Add the white wine to the sauce and cook for 5 minutes more. Strain again, and stir in the butter to make the sauce shiny.

Brown Sauce

(Makes about 4 cups)

¾ cup butter   3 cups beef stock
½ cup flour

Melt the butter in a saucepan over low heat. Add flour gradually, blending well. Cook slowly over low heat, stirring occasionally, until roux is thoroughly blended and brown. Gradually add stock; bring to a boil and cook about 5 minutes, stirring constantly. Lower heat and simmer gently for about ½ hour, stirring occasionally. Skim off fat and strain through fine sieve.

Another Christmas Dinner. This one served twenty-two people.

With cocktails

2 pounds of crab fingers.
About 60. A few were left over.
Hot cheese puffs

Dinner

Boeuf bourguignon

Wine   Cold Polish ham

Château Figeac 1962 Smoked turkey

Noodles String beans

Plum pudding

Pumpkin pie

Coffee Sanka Chocolate peppermints

Champagne with the presents

A third Christmas Dinner for twenty-three

With Cocktails

Pâté de foie gras

Caviar

Hot cheese puffs

Dinner

      Sea-food casserole (Made by Park East,

Pouilly Fuissé   Rice   our fish store. It

                  was delicious.)

Roast turkey with chestnut and oyster

dressing. Dr. Brown officiated.

Château Lynch   Polish ham

Bages 1964   Vegetable salad

Plum pudding Pumpkin pie

Coffee Sanka Chocolate peppermints

Champagne with the presents

I do not like to sail under false colors, and it is only fair to acknowledge that our luxury items, caviar, pâté de foie gras, the champagne, smoked turkey, and Polish ham are usually gifts that generous friends contribute to the Christmas celebration.

Indeed one Christmas Eve I had a brisk run-in with my godson, David Lyall, whose parents had brought along a princely pot of caviar. Young master Lyall was allowed a small taste and he was no fool. Instantaneously acclimating himself to the best things in life which, contrary to the assurance of the popular song, are far from free, he kept hovering around the table on which the caviar was set, sneaking a surreptitious spoonful any time the watchful eye of an adult strayed away from him.

Whenever I see caviar I am reminded of a beau of my Hollywood days. We were dining one night in a posh restaurant and he ordered blinis for dessert, those glorious thin crêpes stuffed with caviar and shrouded in sour cream. They were so delicious that he suggested a second go-round.

When the bill came he studied it and then said to me courteously, "Will you join me in washing dishes in the kitchen? I haven't got enough dough to bail us out of here."

CHAPTER FIVE

Before-the-Theatre Suggestions

So far we have been discussing leisurely dining, but there are of
course those hurried meals before the theatre or the annual ten-
ants' meeting or the game or whatever it may be.

You may not want a lot of food but you do want something
that will stay you. Speaking of theatre, I don't know whether to
be glad or sorry about the change in curtain time in New York's
theatres from eight-thirty to seven-thirty.

With eight-thirty dinner was always rushed, but with seven-
thirty if you don't eat something beforehand you're starving by
nine forty-five.

You can always have a drink and a sandwich, but a bowl of
hearty soup is a good friend too, an added virtue being that
soups come in cans. They are quickly and easily prepared and
when they are good they are very good. A few, not many, but a
few frozen foods are good too and one might as well take advantage of the best of them.

Frozen meat pies are for the most part a fraud. In the chicken
and turkey ones the poultry is usually stringy and tasteless and
although on the whole I have found the beef to be more pleasing,
the amount of meat in both of them is negligible. Potatoes and

carrots abound. Get out Junior's home microscope if you want to find the meat.

A frozen preparation that I do think has taste and substance is Stouffer's creamed chipped beef. Served on toast or a toasted English muffin, it has a lot of flavor and would make a good pre- or after-theatre supper dish just as it makes a good, quick and easy luncheon. And although I am not a tuna-fish buff, I must say I find their frozen tuna noodle casserole very flavorful.

A more sophisticated and truly delicious dish served either for its own sake or as a memorable entree to a formal lunch or dinner I filched from my friend, Bobsie, Mrs. Gilbert Chapman.

Chez Madam Chapman the food is superb, the reason being not only the skill of her cook but the culinary knowledge of Madam herself. Over a period of years the cooks have changed, the caliber of the food remains the same.

The dish is, in essence, a non-sweet jelly-roll cake lined, not with jelly, but a marvelous mushroom mélange. Don't have too much on your mind when you set out to do it because it takes a while and, the first couple of times at least, quite a bit of concentration but guests and family salaam with gratifying reverence when you present it.

When I asked Bobsie if she would be an angel and give me the recipe her acquiescence was immediate. "Of course I will," she said, adding, by way of a subtle boost to my morale, "Alice B. Toklas used three of my recipes too."

I hope I have too much sense to think I am in Miss Toklas' class, although I tangle with that lady on her treatment of sweetbreads, but I just want you to know that we are dealing with top-drawer stuff. Furthermore it is all here.

There are people, sometimes they even include dear friends and almost always they include professional cooks, who will open-handedly give you a recipe, leaving out only that small secret ingredient or knack of combination that makes the dish so special.

It's understandable, they want to hang onto something unique.

I've been tempted myself, but I think it a mean instinct and I try to overcome it. After all, if there's anything in the world you can give away completely without robbing yourself it's a recipe for good food. Herewith then Bobsie Chapman's offering to the betterment of mankind.

Marvelous Mushroom Mélange

(Serves 6–8)

Cake:

Dusting of flour	2 cups milk
¼ cup butter	4 eggs, separated
½ cup flour	1 teaspoon granulated sugar
Pinch of salt	Toasted bread crumbs

Mushroom Filling:

2 medium onions, chopped	3 tablespoons sour cream
¼ cup olive oil	2 tablespoons lemon juice
1 pound mushrooms, finely chopped	2 tablespoons chopped pimiento
3 tablespoons finely chopped scallions	Salt and pepper to taste

To make cake: Preheat oven to 325° F. Oil a jelly-roll pan (10×15 inches). Line with wax paper. Oil the paper and dust lightly with flour. In a saucepan, melt butter; stir in ½ cup flour and the salt. Cook over medium heat, stirring constantly for several minutes. Gradually beat in the milk and cook the sauce, stirring constantly, until it is smooth and very thick. Remove pan from heat. Beat the egg yolks and sugar until pale yellow; stir in the cooked sauce; cool. Fold in the egg whites, which have been beaten until stiff but not dry. Spread the batter evenly in the prepared pan. Bake 40 to 45 minutes, or until it is golden and pulls away from the sides of the pan.

While the cake is baking, make mushroom filling: Sauté onions in olive oil until tender and golden. Add mushrooms and cook mixture over low heat, stirring frequently, until it is dry in texture. Remove the mushroom mixture from heat and stir in the remaining ingredients. You may increase the filling by a small amount and no harm is done.

To assemble: Invert the baked cake immediately after removing from oven onto two overlapping sheets of wax paper which have been sprinkled with the toasted bread crumbs. Remove pan, peel paper from bottom. Slice off hard edges, spread roll with the mushroom filling. Roll cake, starting at long edge, using wax paper as an aid, lifting and rolling the cake gently onto itself. Serve the roll hot with lightly salted sour cream mixed with chopped chives. This would be a super pre-theatre snack.

Before this digression I mentioned soups as satisfactory nourishment before a play, since they will adequately stave off starvation until you can get to a restaurant for dinner or a light supper after the performance.

For one of the best, appropriately enough I am indebted to Selena Royle Renavant, now in the real estate business and domiciled in Guadalajara, Mexico, but once a well-known, talented, and busy leading lady on Broadway.

Until a recent trip to Mexico it was many years since I had seen Selena, but in our hearts we kept a warm spot for one another. Like men who have been companions in arms, we once battled together trying to overcome a script written by one of the great names of the American theatre, Eugene O'Neill. Our battleground was *Days Without End,* a Theatre Guild production, and the going was rough. The play was known to the cast as Daze Without End, and Selena, her then husband Earl Larrimore, Stanley Ridges, and I did our best but much as we regretted being out of jobs we all drew a sigh of relief when a conspicuous lack of customers closed the show.

Selena subsequently married the charming actor Georges Renavant and, until his death, they lived for many happy years in Mexico.

Selena writes about the country she has come to love, and she cooks noteworthy meals for her many friends. When I voiced my enthusiasm for the soup she served when I dined with her one night in Guadalajara, she gave me the recipe and I herewith pass it on.

Selena's Soup

(Serves 8)

2 tablespoons butter	1 cup cooked, diced chicken
¼ cup minced onion	1 cup cooked rice
¼ cup diced celery	½ cup diced green stuffed olives
2 tablespoons flour	½ cup diced black pitted olives
4 cups chicken broth	2 cups light cream, warmed

In large saucepan, melt butter. Add onion and celery and cook until tender and golden. Sprinkle on the flour and keep stirring, slowly adding the chicken broth until well blended. Cook 5 minutes. Then add the chicken, rice, and olives. Mix well. If it is to be served at once, stir in the warmed cream. Otherwise it may be set aside, reheated, and the warm cream added just before serving.

The olives give a piquant unexpected flavor. The soup is rich and filling, but if you do want something else cold, sliced, boiled ham and salad with perhaps a fruit dessert would make an excellent and certainly ample meal.

If you are cutting corners on time and trouble the canned soups are lifesavers. My own favorite in cold weather is black bean. Diluted with beef broth instead of water, heated slowly and stirred pretty constantly to get all the lumps out, enlivened with a generous splash of sherry and with a thin slice of lemon and hard-boiled egg on top, it's delicious.

A nice accompaniment for it and many other soups and salads is crackers treated the way our friend Mrs. Walter Allen used to do them.

Leslie Allen, a vigorous and charming woman, was for many years the doyenne of the Mill Reef Club in Antigua. At noontime the guests she invited eagerly crowded her beach to enjoy her engaging company and to swim in the pellucid waters lapping the sands. They swam, they chatted with friends, and they partook of the delicious rum punches that old Tom, who was with her for so many years, concocted with a master's hand. They also nibbled, like famished mice, the delicious crackers passed around in baskets.

When I asked Leslie what she did to them to make them so special she laughed and said it was a New England recipe that used to appear regularly in old cookbooks. You can do it with two or three kinds of crackers, but by far the first choice is what were called Common crackers; or Boston crackers—thick, biscuitlike affairs often served with clam chowder.

Boston Crackers

Preheat oven to 350° F. Split crackers in half and soak for a few minutes in ice water until soft, but do not let them disintegrate. Drain. Place split side up on pastry sheet. Put 1 teaspoon butter on each cracker and bake in the upper part of the oven for 5 to 8 minutes or until crisp and slightly browned. In an airtight jar they will keep for a week or more.

Uneeda Biscuits may be treated the same way except that they must be left whole, not split.

When I learned about the Uneeda Biscuit choice I was skeptical. It had been a long time since I'd noticed any on grocers' shelves, but the package with the little boy in the yellow slicker was part of my childhood scene. To my delight, I found that the U.B. people are still in business. It was just that I had outgrown my slicker.

CHAPTER SIX

Cocktail Parties

I have few suggestions for these since I attend perhaps two a year and never give them.

There are several reasons for this lack of sociability. One is I don't have a very strong back and standing about for hours wears me out.

The first Queen Elizabeth is reported to have been a great stander and although a light drinker she would probably have felt at ease on the cocktail circuit. She could stand for hours and used to exhaust foreign ambassadors in audience, since none might sit while the Queen stood. Apparently she had a spine of steel instead of the bone and cartilage allotted to lesser mortals.

At cocktail parties there are usually far more people invited than there are chairs to sit on, but even the chairs and sofas available are rarely used and this I think is because people are afraid of being trapped. At a dinner party there is no cause for concern. Inevitably dinner will be announced, and if you are not all that enchanted with your vis-à-vis you will be harmoniously separated. Should any malaise occur at table, that too is short-lived. Dinner will soon be over and you can engage in conversation with another.

But at a cocktail party you are supposed to circulate. If a woman feels cornered she may perhaps say to the man who is boring her to pulp, "I wonder if you'd be nice enough to get me a refill," hand him her glass, and melt into the crowd hoping he won't spot her again. If she is a non-drinker her problem is more acute. Then there is not much she can do other than say, "Excuse me a moment," and break away. If her partner is one of those determined talkers hell-bent on finishing an endless tale she may have to say, "Excuse me a moment, I have to go to the bathroom." Only the coward cringes when desperate measures are necessary.

Men, as is so frequently the case, are better off. A man can ask if he may replenish a lady's glass and then either simply not do so or bring her back the dividend and fade from her side, mission accomplished. If she refuses his offer she should then say, "Thank you, no, but please get something for yourself," and they are both home free.

Another reason I take a dim view of the average cocktail party is that if I am going to be with friends I want to be able to communicate with them and the noise and crowding and shifting about makes this difficult.

Then, too, they are a menace to the dinner hour. If a woman is the family cook, cocktail-party time is just when she should be in the kitchen organizing her preparations for dinner. If children are not involved, a man and wife may simply decide they don't care how late they eat or that they will dine in a restaurant, but if there are children who must be returned to and fed, the party presents a hurdle.

Another snag, although this of course can occur in any gathering, is that you may run into someone whom you know you know but have difficulty in placing and you feel like a fool.

This happened to me one evening at a dinner party. A pretty actress whom I had met casually in our Hollywood days passed near me.

"Hello," I said, "how nice to see you again. How are you?"

She turned. "Oh hello, it's good to see you too," and she

72

flashed a dazzling smile. "It's . . . it's . . . why, it's Ina Claire, isn't it!"

I said, "Yes." As I did so an Oh, God-what-have-I-done expression crossed her face. Knowing the feeling, I tried reassurance. "Never mind," I said, "you were close. The initials are the same."

In a roundabout way it reminded me of people who having seen you on the stage or in television will sometimes come up to you in the street and say, "Now wait a minute, wait a minute, I know you perfectly well. You're . . . you're . . . oh, what *is* your name?" You tell them. "That's right!" and they give you a jab in the arm that nearly knocks you over. Their tone is so congratulatory you feel like the happy, coffee-growing peasants to whom El Exigente gives the nod of approval or as though you had won "Let's Make a Deal" or "Truth or Consequences." Hurray for me, I know my name!

Obviously I am not unaware that there are occasions when the cocktail party does fill a specific need. It is a godsend to those who either are not interested in food or who are simply not organized to offer meals. It is the answer when some kind of a celebration is called for yet the group one wishes to gather together is too large to make dinner feasible.

As a rule these are professional fiestas. A new book has been published or someone has won a Nobel Prize or the home team has brought back the pennant or a politician is being presented to those who, happily, will become adherents and donors.

On the private side, a birthday or a housewarming or an anniversary celebration is in order. Perhaps a friend who lives abroad is home on a brief visit and you want to gather the cronies. These are times when cocktail parties neatly fill the bill, but to my way of thinking they require a specific cause.

Many people go to cocktail parties for the simple reason that they have been invited, I have done so myself, and also because there is always the hope that you just *might* meet somebody interesting. Or perhaps a mutually advantageous contact may be formed. Or it may be that you ask a person or a couple whom you have met only once but liked very much to drop in for a cocktail when you feel or feel *they* might feel that you do not know them well enough to ask them to dine.

In any event, having accepted an invitation it's a good idea to follow it up. Norton and I were one time asked to stop by for a drink on a yacht. It had a glamorous sound, and since the boat would be tied up at the host's dock, boarding presented no problem. If there is anything I am not adept at, it is hooking myself onto a rope ladder let down the side and trying to step from a bobbing dinghy onto the first flexible rung.

One Fourth of July we were invited by our friends the Robert Townsends to a party on a yacht anchored offshore. The same Mr. Townsend whose book *Up the Organization* caused such a stir. We were to meet the other guests, have cocktails, and then everyone would return to the beach club for dinner. Since I was obviously in difficulty trying to clamber aboard, those on deck called down, "Just hold up your arms, we'll pull you up." I did and they did and my right shoulder, which has an unpleasant little trick of quick dislocation, went out of its socket. I let out a shriek, as it is extremely painful.

There I lay writhing on the deck until my husband arrived two or three minutes later in another launch and reset it, an operation he is very good at.

May it never happen to you, but if it should, the way to cure it is to lie flat on the floor (or deck) have someone take off his shoe, insert his heel into your armpit and give a gentle but firm pull to the arm. Snaps right back. The other guests watched the performance with a mixture of awe and bewilderment.

It was a reasonably spectacular entrance. Nor was our departure altogether anticlimactic.

One would think that Norton, having spent sixteen months in the Pacific on board a carrier in World War Two, would be well grounded, or well seaed, in these procedures. Not so, although his difficulties were in reverse. It was when we were debarking that he came a cropper. He had one foot on the last rung of the ladder and was reaching with the other for the gunwale of the dinghy, when the kid who was propelling it swerved from the side of the yacht. Good Dr. Brown dropped kerplunk into the narrow channel thus created.

There was a gasp from the onlookers, but as he is a powerful swimmer I was not too alarmed. He presented quite a picture however as he surfaced, his horn-rim glasses still in place, his pipe still clenched between his teeth.

A truly gallant gesture was made by one Mr. J. Burch Ault, who, seeing Norton drop, instantly ripped off his coat and leaped from the deck into the water to help him. They both emerged safely, but since my loved one was quite moist we decided not to stay for dinner.

I do not know whether our friends the Townsends charter a yacht every Fourth of July, but if they do, we are not asked to the parties.

The other boat I mentioned however was a different proposition. It was tied to the dock so you'd barely know you weren't on dry land. Around six o'clock of a Sunday afternoon we spruced ourselves up and drove to our friend's house. There were a couple of cars in the driveway, but an air of fiesta was lacking. "Everybody's down at the dock," said Norton. "Come on." In a couple of minutes it became apparent that while there was a dock a boat there was not. We wandered around and came upon a pretty girl sunning herself on the lawn.

"Excuse me," I said, "we're sorry to intrude, but is there a party going on here someplace?"

She smiled pleasantly. "I'm afraid not. But there was a big party here yesterday."

I had goofed. I had written it in my engagement book for Sunday when Saturday was *der Tag*. I was abject in my apologies to Norton, but although he regretted having missed the merry-making, I noticed a gleam of amusement in his eye. "Well, well," said he, "even if a party is involved you too are only human. Made a mistake, just like the common people."

A guest or two missing from a cocktail party is of moment chiefly to the missers, although it is courteous either to telephone or write a note saying you are sorry to have defaulted. A missed dinner is much more important. Then notes and flowers along with the sackcloth and ashes is the required procedure. Also an invitation to dine with *you* is not a bad idea.

And sometimes a small group gathered in the early evening can be very nice. We have friends in the country, Admiral and Mrs. Golinkin who occasionally ask in a few people—eight, ten, never more than twelve, and it is pleasant.

In big cities, and especially in New York, with the theatres starting at seven-thirty, cocktail parties serve as a prologue to the evening. You look in on the festivities, have a drink, hopefully a few goodies, and depart for the play. People on their way to a dinner come by in evening dress before going on to the party. If that is the case it is to be hoped they know their own capacity so they do not arrive at the house of their dinner hosts half squiffed.

Speaking of cocktail-party goodies, I am indebted to the learned book of that learned gentleman of food Mr. James Beard for my knowledge of the difference between hors d'oeuvre and canapés. That is the title of his book, and as he writes in the introduction "Outside the meal or, as Mr. Webster puts it, outside the work (his wife must have been a bad cook) has come into our language as the appetizer."

He also quotes from *André Simon's French Cook Book:* "Hors d'oeuvre means 'outside the meal' and regardless of how many different sorts may be provided 'outside' or before any one meal, there is but one meal or oeuvre, so that, in French, oeuvre remains in the singular and hors d'oeuvre never is written hors d'oeuvres."

Strictly speaking, hors d'oeuvre are served without bread or crackers. They may be eaten with a fork or speared on toothpicks.

"Canapé," Mr. Beard continues, "probably comes from the French word that has come to be canopy in English. It means literally, and I again quote Mr. Webster, 'a bed with mosquito netting.' That is fairly accurate, for we have a bed of toast or biscuit or pastry shell, hidden by the 'mosquito netting' of savory butters or pastes or the million and two things used these days for taste bud stimulants."

Hors d'Oeuvre and Canapés, first published by Barrows in 1940, lists literally hundreds of suggestions for spreads and sandwich fillings. I respectfully pass along four that I can vouch for.

Chicken Marron Spread

Purée four or five cooked chestnuts. Mix these with one cup of chopped chicken meat, two tablespoons of finely chopped celery, salt and pepper to taste, and enough mayonnaise to bind.

Hazelnut Spread

Grind ½ pound of toasted salted hazelnuts very fine. Blend these with enough butter to form a thick paste. This is delicious by itself or blended with ham or tongue for a canapé.

Ham and Pineapple Filling

For a sandwich filling you might try chopped ham with sweet gherkin and a little chopped pineapple.

Ham and Chicken Filling

Another delicious one is chopped ham and chopped chicken in equal parts with a few chopped, toasted Brazil nuts mixed with them. Season with English mustard or horseradish.

CHAPTER SEVEN

Weekend Guests

To think of weekend guests is immediately to call to mind that other classic W, weather. When you are in the country, what to do with them if it rains?

Probably in recent years hosts and guests alike were never more put to it than in June 1972 when for about twelve days hurricane Agnes blanketed the eastern part of the nation causing death, untold millions in damage, and unmeasured heartache. On the trivial but still human side, what discombobulation! What wild canceling of parties or, if they were not canceled, what transforming of that which had been envisaged as a fête champêtre into an indoor subway rush hour.

However, while a large outdoor party torpedoed by hostile weather presents a crisis, it is seldom boring.

If, let us say, it is a summer wedding reception or debutante dance there is likely to be a marquee which may be warmed and cheered by cannily placed braziers and the extra help can shelter the guests with umbrellas as they battle their way from car to front door.

The more acute problems arise when house room is limited and you are counting on your terrace or patio to take care of the

79

overflow. Incidentally, when I say terrace and patio I mean two distinct areas, although I realize I am in the minority. I am a member of an ethnic group. In this country, by and large, patio means simply the outdoor space adjacent to a house. It can be a back yard, a front lawn, or what I would call a terrace. When I say patio I mean a courtyard completely surrounded by the house and open to the sky. I mean what the Arabs and Spaniards and Mexicans mean. I do not mean all outdoors.

To my way of thinking a terrace is an extension of the house, a level surface. It may be grass or flagstone or pebbles. It may overlook a sloping lawn or a lake or stream, the Mediterranean or a mountain gorge. It may be bounded by a balustrade or low wall, and on it is placed durable, hopefully waterproof, furniture. But if it is open it is not enclosed and therefore not a patio.

Try explaining that to a seller of "patio" furniture. Not that he's necessarily wrong about his product. What serves the patio can serve the terrace as well, but if you have a feeling for words you find the inaccuracy irritating.

Be that as it may, terrace or patio, if you need them to take care of the party overflow when they are blotted out by rain, all your ingenuity is called into play placing tables and removing certain pieces of furniture to make way for people. Yet there again, you may be squashed but you are not bored. It's when you have plenty of room and only two or at the outside three or four weekend guests that your wits may begin to wither.

No matter how dear they are, or what good sports or how fond you are of each other, they start to get restless. They give you dark looks as though, in some abstruse way, you was responsible for the inclemency.

Should you have a young, newly married or newly entranced couple on your hands, they can have happy times closeted in the guest room, but come the middle ages and the antiquities, what to do?

Norton and I are blessed in having a beach of our own and it is wonderful to see friends reveling in sun, sand, and water, weather permitting.

It is when I see the glory and happiness of sunshine and the gloom and discouragement induced by prolonged rain that I am appalled by the thought that governments of all nations are tinkering with weather. Seeding clouds to induce rain in time of drought is one thing. Doing it to harass, dishearten, flood out, and eventually, in unmatched callousness, destroy the people of another country is despicable.

Wars were terrible when limited to the clash of army against army. When the entire civilian population of a country is victimized, as was the case with the American invasion of Vietnam and the American bombing of Cambodia, they are intolerable.

That's one thing you can do on a rainy weekend: discuss the horrors of war. But there are more enjoyable pastimes too. Bridge players will take to cards. If the house boasts a billiard table, hooray! Even amateurs can have fun with that one.

There is always television and while still, for the most part, Mr. Newton Minnow's vast wasteland, *somewhere* the sun is shining and *that* where there will be a baseball game. When it is conjured onto the screen with happy exclamations by my husband or a guest my heart sinks, because I find it very boring, and while I do not have to watch it I know that unless I close every door behind me, the sound of the announcer's voice will follow me wherever I go in my house.

Once in a great while Norton or I will tentatively—and then only after assurances that if they don't like the idea our guests will, cross their hearts and hope to die, say so—suggest showing some of the slides he has taken in our travels around the world. Once in a while we meet with a genuinely enthusiastic response. There are those who would like to see Tahiti or the wild game of Africa or, on a gray and rainy day, the sun-drenched isles of Greece.

Sometimes, should you have a collection of old records, it's a lot of fun to unearth and play them. Musical scores, single songs, and a sampling of the great talk albums. Flanders and Swann, Bob Newhart, Tom Lehrer, Abe Burrows, the classic *Songs of Couch and Consultation* with Katie Lee singing the lyrics and music of Bud Freeman and Leon Pober, or, for serious drama lovers, the recorded achievements of John Gielgud and Laurence Olivier. I have nothing against Simon and Garfunkel either, but those milestones along memory lane induce a wondrous nostalgia, and even young guests find them groovy. Almost as if you'd gotten yourself up in bustles or leg-of-mutton sleeves.

There is also an extraordinary album, *The Language and Music of the Wolves.* It is produced by the editors of *Natural History Magazine,* which is published by the American Museum of Natural History, and is a recording of wolf barks and howls taped during three seasons in Algonquin Park, Canada.

It is an eerie, forlorn, primeval wail of living creatures who are being extinguished by the brutality and stupidity of man. On the back of the album envelope are notes by Charles Burr in which he states that the ". . . wolf howls today are . . . a kind of swan song . . . Men hunt them by airplane and snowmobile. Soon they will be another of the growing number of extinct species.

"The wolf kills to eat . . . we kill *him* for sport and out of unreasoning terror. In killing them we are proclaiming that no animal in nature has a right to live except ourselves."

The recorded cries are thrilling. A sound so ancient that hairs rise on the back of the neck and the subconscious stirs with memories of an unrecognized and long forgotten heritage.

For those who are interested in these superb beasts and who would like to know the truth about them rather than believe the manufactured legends of their ferocity, I recommend the following books: David L. Mech's *The Wolf: The Ecology and Behavior of an Endangered Species* (Natural History Press), and Douglas H. Pimlott and Russel J. Rutters' *The World of the Wolf* (Lippincott), also *Never Cry Wolf* by Farley Mowat, published by the Dell Publishing Co., and *Arctic Wild* by Lois Crisler, published by Harper and Brothers.

Mrs. Crisler and her husband, like Mr. Mowat, lived for an extended period in close association with wolves and all three found the difference between reputation and reality to be almost incredible. Indeed as Mr. Mowat says, "Inescapably the realization was being borne in upon my preconditioned mind that the centuries-old and universally accepted human concept of wolf character was a palpable lie. On three separate occasions in less than a week I had been completely at the mercy of these 'savage killers' but far from attempting to tear me limb from limb they had displayed a restraint verging on contempt, even when I invaded their home and appeared to be posing a direct threat to the young cubs."

But to return to our rainy weekend. Jigsaw puzzles still have their enthusiastic adherents, and although I find the cardboard ones distasteful—it is like giving a child a plastic bucket instead of an authentic wooden one to play with in the sand—those that *are* cut from real wood, if they're very complicated, are challenging and fun.

A couple of books of Double-Crostics are a good refuge from boredom for many people, as are one or two sets of Playplax. Granted, the colored rings and squares which fit together are made from Polystyrene, which has got to be a derivative of plastic, but they are sturdy, and grownups as well as children, for whom they were originally designed, can flex their imaginations and inventiveness.

One rainy weekend, when our friends the Zieglers were with us, Jimmy, who having retired from medical research has developed his inherent talent not only for painting but for art in every medium, put together an abstract arrangement that was so decorative that I kept it intact for a long time and used it as a centerpiece for the dinner table.

Another rainy-day pastime I would also propose is a waning yet once popular pursuit, reading. We have a great many books, and while I am mean about lending them out—I would far rather give a friend a book than lend it—in my own home he is more than welcome to ravage the shelves.

And then, and this venture is truly ideal in bad weather—always supposing of course that friend's enthusiasm matches one's own—there is cooking.

In a fully staffed house it is perhaps more prudent if the help are given the day off should the mistress and her guests plan on taking over the kitchen, but in an informal household dear Elisabeth or Katherine or Emma may allow her domain to be invaded if she is certain that the amateurs will clean up after themselves. Hopefully, too, her ego will be bolstered as she watches the shambles the poor slobs are creating.

But it isn't fair to any cook or housekeeper to soil a lot of pots and pans and expect her to clean them up. And while on that track, a day off should be a day off, not sandwiched in between two days of double duty: one preparing food in advance for a helpless employer, the day after cleaning up the disorder the employer has created.

This I think is fair and a sound philosophy but it does depend to some extent on the employee. My mother once had working for her a superb woman named Fanny Feister who was Hungarian. She was devoted to Mother, she respected her, and while she understood that Mother's job as editor-in-chief of *Vogue* was a distinguished one, it did not occur to Fanny that her employer had much housekeeping ability. Nor was she altogether wrong. A day with my mother in the kitchen was not unlike Miss Katherine Hepburn's famous cooking sequence in *Woman of the Year.*

Every day before her day off and indeed early in the morning thereof, Fanny would be cooking and baking and preparing salad dressing and setting the table so that all my mother and Dick Newton, my stepfather, had to do was get stuff out of the icebox and perhaps pop a casserole in the oven.

Mother, who was eminently successful in her own field, regarded Fanny's achievements as something of a miracle. She herself had a repertory of dishes she could cook. There were three of them, and they were excellent, but on the whole she felt about cooking as I feel about music. I think it's marvelous and to me musicians are a special race but I do not understand the notes or how to set them down or read them nor how to transcribe into sound what is written on the paper.

Mother and Dick were quite good about cleaning up after

themselves, but Fanny wasn't any too seduced by that performance either. They never put things back in their accustomed places.

Mother was devoted to her cook and gave her pretty presents; clothes, ornaments for her room, whatever she thought she might like, but Fanny always laid them carefully away. She said they were too nice to use. This used to irk mother and she would grumble to me about it. I would try to smooth her feathers by saying something like, "Darling, don't fret. That's Fanny's way of enjoying those nice things."

"But it's not mine," wailed my unsmoothed parent. Mother was a generous woman, to me exceedingly so, but she was not extravagant, and money spent to no better purpose than to be laid away in a bureau drawer harassed her. Or, as I used to say as a child when something upset me, "It guts me to the bone."

If Fanny was simply going to "lay it away" mother would have preferred giving her ten or twenty dollars to put in the savings bank.

Fanny loved being in the country and early on summer mornings and in the evenings she would walk barefoot in the dew on the grass as she had done in Europe as a girl.

When *A Tree Grows in Brooklyn* was a big movie hit, Mother and Dick went to see it and when she came home Mother said, "Oh Fanny, we've just been to a wonderful picture. You must go to see it on your day off. It's about a poor little girl growing up in Brooklyn and you can't think how good it is."

Fanny smiled, but Mother sensed she had not touched a chord. "You'd enjoy it," she urged. "I'm sure you would." Fanny shook her head tolerantly. "No, madam," she said, "I do not care to see pictures about poor people. When I was a girl in Hungary I worked for the *baronen*. I lived in castles, and great carriages drew up at the door and people in beautiful clothes got out and came to dinner and that is the kind of life that interests me. Not poor people."

"I see," said my mother, murmuring a prayer of gratitude that this aristocracy buff lived in her comparative hovel and was willing to stay there.

One of Mother's specialties mentioned above was a marvelous creamy rice pudding. Another was cranberry pie. As a child my mother had lived with her grandparents in Budtown, in those days a hamlet in New Jersey. My great-grandfather, a teacher who had immigrated from Indiana, kept the village store, so cranberries were no problem.

I watched my mother bake the pie several times, but when I wanted to set the recipe down in this book I found my conception of it was nebulous. "What to do, what to do?" I groaned and I moaned and then I received a Sign. It was like that hand that emerges from a man's cuff, the index finger pointing. I received from Atheneum, publishers of an old family friend, June Platt, a copy of her seventh contribution to human pleasure, *June Platt's New England Cook Book*.

Although June and her late husband, Joe, were much younger than my mother they, Mother, and I were good friends. Joseph Platt was an artist and scenic designer. Among his credits were the sets for the movie *Gone With the Wind*. He also created an elegant and charming décor for my dramatization of my novel *In Bed We Cry*. I should have let well enough alone. The novel was successful. The play was a resounding flop, but Joe's reviews were fine. During my mother's editorial span at *Vogue*—she spent her life with the magazine and was its editor for thirty-eight years—June and Joe contributed to it as well as to *House & Garden*, another Condé Nast publication.

June Platt has always been a great cook, and when I first knew her she was certainly one of the prettiest, with bright blue eyes, short blond curly hair, and a skin like flower petals. She was also the mother of two sons who grew to be high and healthy largely as a result of the meals contrived by little Mum. In a way their wives are to be sympathized with, because if those boys say of a dish set before them, "Honey, this is not like what Mother used to make," they are only speaking gospel.

Anyway, licking my lips in ladylike fashion as I was leafing through Mrs. Platt's latest endeavor, what did my happy eyes fall upon but a recipe for cranberry pie.

Knowing that June and Mother had been good friends I thought, Who was the chicken, who the egg in this enterprise? Did Mother tell June about it or did she perhaps say something like, "You know, June, when I was growing up my grandmother made the most delicious cranberry pie, but I don't quite remember how she went about it"? And did June say "Perhaps it was this way," and give her the recipe?

Having tossed these suppositions around for a while I thought, This is crazy. Why don't I *ask* June? A call to her publisher elicited her address. I wrote to her and the day she received my letter she telephoned me from the Pennsylvania town where she is now living.

We picked up a few threads, talked of old times, and by this pleasant and circuitous route came at last to the pie.

"The only thing is, June," I said, "I remember Mother making a cross in the top crust and folding it back and pouring in molasses as it cooked. I think your recipe doesn't say that."

"No," she said, "you're right. This one is a little different. The one that Edna (my ma) used to make is the one Sophie Kerr and I put in the cookbook we did together, *The Best I Ever Ate*."

"May I use it?" I begged.

"Of course you may. Go ahead and good luck."

Herewith, courtesy of Edna Woolman Chase, June Platt, Sophie Kerr, and, I suppose, if one is being thorough, my Quaker great-grandmother Mrs. Joseph Burr Woolman, a delicious dessert.

Use your favorite pie pastry, making enough for two crusts. The one given here is June Platt's.

Cranberry Pie

(Serves 6–8)

Pie crust:

2½ cups pastry or all-purpose flour

1 teaspoon salt

6 tablespoons vegetable shortening

6 tablespoons butter

3–6 tablespoons ice water

Cranberry filling:

4 cups fresh cranberries

1¼ cups light brown sugar, firmly packed

3 tablespoons molasses

2 tablespoons water

Preheat oven to 425° F. To make the pastry: Sift the flour and salt into a bowl and work the vegetable shortening and butter into it with your fingertips. When mealy in consistency, moisten with ice water, adding a small amount at a time. Form into two balls, one slightly larger than the other. It may be used immediately, but some cooks prefer to wrap it in wax paper and chill it for a little while. Take the smaller ball of pastry, roll it out, and line your pie plate. Mrs. Platt has a very professional way of doing this. She says, "Roll out to about ⅛ of an inch thickness, keeping dough in a circular shape.

"To lift into the pan, place the rolling pin crosswise at the top of the circle, lift the top of the pastry, and hold it against the pin. Then, roll the pin toward you, rolling the pastry up onto the pin as you go. Unroll onto the pie plate so the pastry completely covers it. Let it settle well down into the pan before you trim off the excess pastry with floured scissors, leaving about ½-inch hanging over the edge."

Wash and pick over carefully the raw cranberries and cut them in half, one by one. Fill the unbaked pie shell with the cranberries and 1 cup of the sugar. Trickle over all 2 generous tablespoons of the molasses. Now cover with the top crust "which you will roll out in the same way as the bottom, but make the circle slightly larger and moisten the rim of the lower crust before placing the top one on it. When it is in place, cut off the excess at the same point as the lower crust. Press the edges together and roll them under, so as to make a thick edge, then with fingers or fork, crimp the edges together."

Now make a 1½-inch crosslike incision in the center of the top crust and roll back the four flaps, forming a fairly large, square hole in the center. Prick the rest of the surface of the pie all over with a floured fork.

Bake for 10 minutes; reduce heat to 325° F. Combine the remaining ¼ cup brown sugar, 1 tablespoon molasses, and water in saucepan and boil for a few minutes. Bake the pie for 1 hour, adding liquid about every 15 minutes in the center hole. The pie when done should be moist and syrupy inside and the bottom crust should be almost caramelized on the bottom. Serve warm accompanied by heavy cream or rat-trap cheese or both. This is super food any time and great at Thanksgiving if you want to stick to convention but have had it with cranberry sauce.

June Platt's New England Cook Book also has the rice pudding I mentioned, the important trick, as Mother used to tell me, being the continued stirring in of the brown skin as it forms on top.

The third dish I so enjoyed we used to have for luncheon when I was home from boarding school on weekends. Mother served it with baked sweet potatoes. I thought it good then and I think it good today.

Mixed Grill

(Serves 4)

4 large *or* 6 small tomatoes	1 cup milk, scalded
Flour	8 small sausages
Salt and pepper	8 slices bacon
4 tablespoons butter	4 French loin lamb chops
2 tablespoons flour	

Leaving the skin on, cut tomatoes in half and gently squeeze out the seeds and watery juice. Slice tomatoes; dip in flour which has been seasoned with the salt and pepper. Sauté 2 to 3 minutes in 2 tablespoons of the butter in a large skillet. When tomatoes are cooked, but still intact, carefully remove from skillet and keep warm.

In skillet, melt remaining 2 tablespoons butter over low heat. Add flour gradually, blending well without browning. Add the warm milk, stirring constantly. Continue to cook and stir until smooth. Simmer for another 5 minutes, and continue to stir, over low heat, to avoid an uncooked flour flavor. Season to taste with salt and pepper. Keep warm while you fry the bacon and sausages. The chops may be either pan-fried or broiled. When everything is done, put the meat in center of a platter with tomatoes at either end. Pour white sauce over tomatoes.

As a change from eggs the fried tomatoes with bacon only is a tempting breakfast dish. Another good way to use up some of what appears to be a hundred thousand glowing globes when your own garden tomatoes are ripe and flourishing is the following.

Baked Tomatoes

(Serves 4)

8 tomatoes	Salt
2 medium onions, chopped	Pepper
1 tablespoon brown sugar	1 to 2 tablespoons butter

Preheat oven to 325° F. Butter well a 2- to 3-quart shallow baking dish. Leaving the skin on, cut tomatoes in quarters. Gently squeeze out the seeds and place cut side up in the prepared dish. Sprinkle with the chopped onions, brown sugar, salt and pepper to taste, and dot with butter.

Bake 1½ to 2 hours or until the tomatoes are almost caramelized. Watch carefully, for they char rather easily. You may have to add a small amount of boiling water from time to time.

There was a time when I used to try to think up original Saturday and Sunday breakfasts when we had weekend guests.

I finally gave up. Now guests are lucky to get coffee or tea, bacon, eggs, toast, assorted jams, and orange juice. The reason being the differences in matutinal tastes and the hours kept.

We inherited our house in the country and there are certain architectural limitations we must accept, but were I building from scratch there are two features I would definitely incorporate in the plan.

One: the guest room would be at the end of a hall so it would be to some extent isolated from household activities and Two: it would include a tiny kitchenette or cooking closet with running water, the smallest available icebox, electric outlets, and a burner.

That way if the guests wanted to sleep until high noon and then get themselves a cup of coffee or even a complete blue-plate special, they could do so. With a sink and running water they could also clean up after themselves and not upset the household routine.

The hostess could have breakfast in bed, if she's accustomed to that, at the time that best suits her. The host, if so minded, could be up at dawn and out in his garden or puttering in his darkroom or whatever, without keeping one eye peeled making sure that dear friends are well provided for.

Because make no mistake. Weekend breakfasts have to be overseen. A cook who may be capable of preparing and getting to the table a fairly involved dinner for eight, deliquesces when it comes to setting a breakfast table for two or four.

In the course of a reasonably long life I have had the usual procession of reasonably able or disabled cooks and I have never known one who could organize the butter *and* the jams *and* the cutlery *and* the cups and plates and the food required for even relatively prosaic breakfasts.

Now, I will say, we have got it reduced to a fairly low and easy denominator. The large coffeepot is plugged in on the sideboard, the four-slice toaster is plugged in beside it. The bread is on a covered plate. Jams, jellies, and marmalades are on the table in their pots, spoons adjacent. Sugar is at hand. So far so good, and in cold weather it works pretty well, but on hot mornings you can't have out the butter and cream and orange juice. They must be kept in the fridge.

If the weekend guests are family or very close friends, they of course can help themselves but sometimes the atmosphere is not all that informal. In this event either the cook or the master or mistress has got to be on tap. If eggs and bacon are requested they must be prepared.

If the house party is lunching out, none of this presents much of a problem, but if luncheon is to be at home, with possibly other guests coming in, late risers complicate matters. Hence my dream of the kitchenette.

Yet weekends well worked out can be extremely pleasant interludes. The time span, now long honored, is usually from Friday afternoon until after dinner or supper Sunday night.

In English country houses before automobiles became so ubiquitous, invitations were frequently issued giving you the time the train left Charing Cross or Waterloo or whatever the station might be on Friday afternoon *and* the time it left Little Squeeking to return to London either Sunday night or *very* early Monday morning at the latest.

Invitations now are usually more flexible, but Sunday night is still a good time to plan on leaving. The traffic I know about best, through grim experience, is that of Long Island and, to a lesser extent, Connecticut, but we have found that between eight-thirty and nine-thirty in the evening the rush has pretty well thinned out and one can return to New York in a reasonable time without the tedious, exasperating *crawling* bumper to bumper which is the inevitable fate of those leaving in the late afternoon in good weather.

We are lucky because I usually drive to the country ahead of Norton and when he comes out Friday afternoon he can have the pleasure of the company of any guests he brings. As a convenience for everybody they drive back to town with him Sunday night. On the occasions when he decides he will stay over and leave at 5:45 on Monday morning, which is literally the hour he does leave, they usually make other plans. It is understandable.

One day I was comparing notes with Ruth Anderson, the friend who was with us on the Lindblad photographic safari through Botswana and South-West Africa that I wrote about in *Worlds Apart*. I said that no matter how much fun you'd been having, if you had a job to do on Monday and your friends did too, it was better if the party broke up Sunday night.

"God, yes," said Mrs. Anderson feelingly. "Even if you're not going to do anything but sit around and moan you want to be alone to do it." Mrs. A. has a large house and entertains frequently and open-handedly and her emotions are strong.

Let us say however that it is a lovely summer Friday and you are Expecting. You will of course check the guest room or rooms. Are there enough hangers in the closet? Note especially pants hangers. There always seems to be a dearth of them and now that the old gag "she wears the pants" had literally come true, they are a necessity.

Clean towels in the bathroom, a bath mat and rubber mat for the tub. You don't want guests slipping and breaking a leg. Fresh soap in the dishes. An extra roll of toilet paper. Bath oil or bath salts, a shower cap, talcum powder, Kleenex. A copy or two of *Reader's Digest* makes satisfactory bathroom reading. As do mail-order catalogues. They're the best! Since I am married to a doctor, we don't go in much for individual pharmacopoeias. If anyone gets ill he is on call, but a few basics I do provide in the medicine chest. Aspirin, bicarbonate of soda. Band-Aids, absorbent cotton, hand lotion, after shave lotion, a razor, toothpaste and a new toothbrush. The latter items have been there for years. A guest has yet to forget his own.

In the room itself, fresh flowers. If possible a plant in winter. If one can manage a small TV set, that is living high on the hog, but a modest radio is not prohibitive and people often like to get the news or dress and undress to music. Ash trays and matches. A clock of course and in winter electric blankets on the beds are deliciously cozy. So too are baby pillows.

Should your guest room boast an open fireplace be sure the fire is laid and that there are extra logs and kindling.

Books. Short stories, essays, collected pieces are best. A paperback copy of *Alice in Wonderland*. But keep that one chained to a bedpost. People are forever saying, "My God, I'd forgotten how enchanting it is" and they tend to secrete it in their luggage when they leave.

If any one brings a dog or cat, for your own sake, along with a bowl of water provide newspapers and a pan of sand. You may also have occasion to be glad you had the foresight to set out a bottle of white vinegar and a bottle of soda; helpful to the carpet in moments of crisis.

The above check list may seem rather long, but after a little while it comes automatically. With a blow of the eye, as the French have it, you can discern if anything is lacking or out of place.

Let us suppose your friends will be arriving around teatime. In hot weather I enjoy iced tea and I have found that many others do too.

In that handsome book, *A Treasury of Great Recipes* compiled by Mary and Vincent Price, the Prices give an elaborate recipe for iced tea using four varieties. It is delicious, but there is also a simple, homey version that is very nice. I have been drinking iced tea all my life but the way Bertha Rose makes it—the fish chowder lady, remember?—is, I think, especially good. Mrs. Rose also eats solids but these two fluid recipes are worth trying.

Tea

For hot tea I prefer Formosa Oolong or Earl Grey or occasionally Lapsang Suchong—all mixed together they form a potent and refreshing brew—but somehow they never seem so successful when iced. For iced tea give me good old Lipton's or an equivalent.

Put into a bowl sugar—the amount must be your own decision, depending on how sweet you like your tea—and a handful of fresh mint leaves. Crush the leaves into the sugar to extract the flavor. Cut 2 lemons in half, squeeze the juice over the mint and sugar, and drop in the rinds. Then add 8 teaspoons of loose tea or 8 tea bags and pour 2 quarts of boiling water over everything. Let steep until the mixture takes on the color you feel will make for satisfactory strength. About ½ teaspoon of powdered ginger or ½ cup of ginger ale adds a subtle fillip. Serve very cold with a sprig of fresh mint in the glass.

Very thin cucumber or tomato or watercress sandwiches and crisp cookies are a pleasant accompaniment to either hot or iced tea.

After tea the chances are your guests will want to unpack. Some like to be sequestered during the operation and firmly close the bedroom door. Others, more sociably inclined, sing out to you to come in and like you to sit on the edge of the bed while they lay away their gear and often they will ask your advice as to which they should wear tonight and which tomorrow.

One can't always gauge one's guests' preferences, but we try for a combination of relaxation and mild sociability.

The routine will vary, but usually our Friday night is for unwinding after a long week in the mines and as a rule we are only the house guests and ourselves for dinner.

Saturdays are flexible, depending on whim, weather, and hobbies. We are stymied if we have golfers, since our club boasts no course, but tennis we can provide and our beach in summer is a great magnet.

It is curious. One may be able to provide a stretch of lawn and a superb mountain view and yet people will become jaded, whereas they can lie on the beach for hours, sifting sand through toes and fingers, watching the water, their eyes following the passing sails. It is, I suppose, racial memory wafting us back several million years.

Sometimes we may be asked out. I always hope we will be for one meal at least and for two reasons. It lightens the burden in the kitchen and it's pleasant for the guests to get around a bit and see other houses.

Sometimes of course there may be reasons why it's not practical, but as a rule if good friends ask you to lunch or dine and you say you are having house guests they will say, "By all means bring them along."

But remember, reciprocity is the key. "We'll ask you and yours this time if you'll ask us and ours the next."

Affection is all very well, congenial companionship sweet, but "Get them out of the house" is the rallying cry ringing through the glens from hostess to hostess. On the other hand, if they don't say "Bring them along," you can't go.

And while on the subject of invitations, one would think that a certain inherent courtesy would keep ladies, quote, unquote, from asking a friend to a party in the presence of a friend whom they are *not* asking. Such behavior seems peculiar, to say the least, but I can't be the only one who has seen it happen. And not only seen it ! Experienced it.

Furthermore, piling Pelion on Ossa, these sensitive souls will tell you of all the guests they *are* inviting or shower you with a detailed account of the wonderful party they have just given. Perhaps you may not want to or cannot attend the bash, but who doesn't like to be asked?

Sometimes of course there may come an occasion when a friend whom you invite is entertaining several people. If a hostess is game to accept them she can have an instant wall-to-wall party without the effort of making a lot of phone calls.

Even if there is no house party going on, there is one slight dilemma faced by those accustomed to entertaining if they accept an invitation to a meal during weekends. If, a couple of weeks ahead of time, the Farthingales, who live only a hoot and a holler away, ask you to dine on Saturday night and you accept, it is awkward if, a little later, you decide you would like to have house guests. You must then first call the Farthingales, and if they say they're sorry but they can't accommodate them, the friends you had in mind miss out on a country weekend and you miss their society because of one meal.

But that's life. You can't have it both ways. I do remember an occasion when we had accepted a Friday night dinner invitation and subsequently invited a couple who are two of our oldest friends. To them we simply said, "Look kids, Elisabeth will give you a good dinner and we'll be home early. Is that all right?" Their little faces positively glowed with pleasure. Service and tranquillity.

But to continue our weekend routine. Whether we have lunched with friends or in our own house an after-luncheon occupation to which we are by no means antagonistic is the siesta.

To my ever renewed surprise, most of our friends are apparently of southern European extraction, relishing a genteel snooze in the afternoon. I am happy to have them knit up the raveled sleeve but more so if they remember to turn down the bedspread before tossing their dressed torsos and shod feet upon it.

Usually we organize a small dinner party for Saturday night, the number varying between six and twelve. It is a pleasant way for close friends who may be with you frequently to meet again your neighbors whom they have met before or, if you get in new blood, to broaden their scope.

In this context I should like to deliver a brief and I daresay obvious little homily, and yet is is something that is often ignored.

Let us say that through friends you meet others with whom you feel instantly compatible. You and they would very much like to meet again. Good! It turns out to be a happy coup for one and all.

There is however a courteous bit of protocol which I feel should be adhered to. If, having met the Cunninghams at the Grandersons' and taken a shine to them, you would like to have them for a drink or dinner, the friendly way to go about it is to call Cookie Granderson, ask if they can come to dinner next Tuesday, and add, "By the way, we liked the Cunninghams so much we'd like to have them too. Do you think it would be all right if I asked them?"

Cookie obviously says yes and what may be a lifelong friendship is launched. You are of course free to branch out on your own and ask them directly, but the Grandersons will inevitably learn of it and a wee little jealousy may raise its head, souring an until now happy relationship.

Another summer weekend occupation is boating. As of this

writing Norton has a Boston whaler. It looks like a large bathtub, but is a seaworthy craft with an outboard motor, and *theoretically* he takes us aboard and we go slurping about the Sound. Very enjoyable. Sometimes it actually happens, but since our outdoor help is only part-time and not all that professional, many of my husband's weekend hours are spent spraying and cultivating and weeding and the boat bobs at its mooring.

Sundays are probably more of the same, although since the yacht club to which we belong serves a very good buffet, we frequently go there for supper. It is a pretty place with a charming harbor view and our friends usually enjoy it. Then back to the house, pack up, and *au revoir*. They all take off for the city, the master at the wheel. I retire to bed with a book or a Double-Crostic, at which I am not good. I have friends who run through the toughest in an hour, but although I am not in their league I enjoy the challenge.

CHAPTER EIGHT

The Shoe on the Other Foot

There is one quite irritating thing to be said about people who live in a city and have a house in the country too. They never want to leave it to spend a weekend with you in your house.

True, invitations to do so are rare, everyone knowing how everyone else feels, but occasionally an offer does pop up.

In our house if this happens and I relay the news to my husband he looks at me as though I had gone daft.

"You mean go *away* for the weekend?"

"Well, dear, that's what Dody said. She said she and Louis would love to have us for the weekend."

"I see. And how's the work in the garden supposed to get done?" Or the storm windows or the screens put up or the new outboard motor secured to the boat or . . . but you get the idea.

If the moon is blue, the man just *may* agree. "Why not?" he will say with disarming amiability. I can count on one finger the number of times it has happened. Long trips, yes. Once we were out of the country for three months, and we have frequently been away for a month or six weeks but that's very different from going away for a *weekend*. A weekend is kind of a sacred time.

This point of view doesn't hold when we are abroad. In a foreign land it's wonderful when friends invite us for the weekend, or any other time. In Europe such outings are especially enjoyable, as very frequently there are small, charming local inns where one may go for a delicious meal. There are a few exceptions, but by and large their counterparts do not exist in the United States. By and large, with the exception of the exorbitantly priced, United States restaurant food is absolutely frightful when it isn't banal.

Another plus about going to a pub or café, especially should your visit be somewhat protracted, is that it gives you, the guest, an opportunity to foot the bill for a change. This may require a combination of guile and brute strength but it *can* be managed.

I am speaking here of the normal folk one is likely to know and assuming everyone is roughly in the same financial bracket. There are occasions, however, when a guest would be ill-advised to suggest a little local outing.

I am reminded of a time Norton and I were invited to spend the weekend in a house which, while in this country, was on a scale not too unlike Bowood, the Wiltshire seat of the Marquess of Lansdowne. It was huge and beautiful, the building superb, the grounds superber.

The owners were an elderly couple since gone to their rest. They are probably a bit disappointed in heaven since it can't possibly be up to what they were accustomed to.

They were kindly people; thoughtful of others, dull, and admirably catered to by a multitudinous and highly paid staff. There is much to be said for life in a house run by well-trained servants, and one of the comments is that today such establishments are as rare as an honorable American President. Another thing you can say is that they can be quite boring.

The system is feasible if the owners are actively engaged in work or hobbies. If they are writers or artists or musicians; if they oversee the estate in professional fashion or are constantly on the golf course or tennis court or cruising the Sound or, like the ducal owners of many of the great English houses, counting the gate and showing sightseers around. But if you are a guest in one of those palazzos and there is literally nothing to do, time hangs heavy.

As my husband had been busy in his office and at the hospital we only arrived late Saturday afternoon. Usually the guests' first occupation, after perhaps a spot of tea, is to unpack.

In that house, needless to say, this prosy detail was taken care of by a maid assigned to me and a valet to Norton. I am not too ardent a fan of the system, as in the few houses we visit where it prevails I can never find anything. Also there is the unsettling suspicion that the maid is comparing your underpants with the lingerie of last week's guests and guess who is the loser? In our own house such little worries never occur. Our friends unpack themselves.

After tea, on this occasion, the time was filled pleasantly enough by being shown over the house, no brief tour by the way, and changing for dinner which, served with pomp and ceremony, was delicious.

Early bed seemed appropriate enough. Our hosts normally retired about half-past nine and Norton, after a busy week, was tired. We slept well in superb beds and awoke to Sunday morning. Like many men my husband would as soon be served hemlock as breakfast in bed. He accordingly dressed and went downstairs. I rang for a tray which appeared exquisitely set with finest napery and subtle food.

I then showered and dressed and went to join the others. It was a lovely morning, so walking around the grounds was a pleasure. We admired the manicured lawns—were you to have said crab grass, those people would have thought it was a dirty word in a foreign tongue—and gazed enviously at the glowing, weedless flower beds.

I often think sadly of forests decimated by the American press, but the destruction seemed almost excusable when we returned to the terrace and the amplitude of the Sunday papers. The New York *Times*, the *Sunday News*, and, in those days, the sturdy *Herald Tribune*. They were three fat time fillers and it took well over a couple of hours to consume them.

Having gone to bed so early we had awakened about eight. It was now noon. Luncheon was to be at one-thirty and no other guests were expected. After lunch the afternoon stretched ahead of us and then Sunday supper. Our hosts had been insistent that we *must* spend the whole day.

What to do? In that household you couldn't very well offer to scrape the carrots or help with the dishes. Despite the wealth there were no diversions such as a swimming pool or ping-pong table. I caught Norton's eye and my expression must have been woebegone. He excused himself, disappeared for a few minutes, and came back looking like the Cheshire cat.

Conversation was desultory, time dragged by, and at last cocktails were served and then a delicious lunch. We went out on to the terrace for coffee and I heard faintly the peal of the telephone. In a moment the butler appeared. Dr. Brown was wanted on the phone. My husband is not a swift mover, but for him he hurried, nay, he scampered. He returned greatly distressed. It had been the hospital calling. One of his patients had just been admitted in emergency condition. The young resident, although hating to have to intrude on his weekend, was urging him to return to town at once.

Our hosts were upset by this sorry interruption, but they understood a physician's duty. Doctors are not the richest men but sometimes they are privileged. The staff rallied, we were packed in a trice, and we departed, waving farewells and promising a speedy return visit. We had played a rather shabby trick on a pair of kindly old bores and we felt like worms. Free, exultant worms.

Another time when we committed a sacrilege by leaving home for a weekend was on a different scale and was a lot more fun.

We spent a weekend with Marya Mannes, the distinguished writer.

Many years ago Marya was on Mother's staff at *Vogue* and our friendship goes back a long way. Norton too feels that Marya is special so she had better not ask us to do anything if she doesn't mean it. We say yes.

The time I refer to we went to visit her in her house on the south shore of Long Island. It is one of the best-designed small houses I have ever seen and I and the Women's Liberation movement are happy to hear that it is the work of a woman architect, Tina Fredericks.

Not only is it attractive, it is comfortable and eminently workable. Marya's friends are stimulating and her wine and food, most of which she cooks herself, are delicious. She is a civilized woman.

One of the best dishes she served was a ham. Actually, since our number was small, half a ham. I no longer remember who it was but a profound scholar voiced one of life's great truths: "Eternity is a ham and two people." Nearly everyone, possibly excepting Mrs. Robert Kennedy and her pullulating clan, has had occasion to ponder this inescapable verity.

I will say however that with Marya's way of doing it, so much of it disappears that you're not likely to have left over more than will make a couple of sandwiches and maybe stuff a pepper.

Marya's Half a Ham

(Serves 6–8)

Half a processed or oven-ready ham
Whole cloves
2 cups firmly packed brown sugar
2–3 tablespoons honey
¼ cup bourbon
1 can (8½ ounces) crushed pineapple, well drained

Preheat oven to 350° F. Wipe ham with damp cloth and place fat side up, in a roasting pan. Bake for 1 hour. Remove from oven, score fat into diamond shapes, and insert a clove in each diamond. Combine remaining ingredients to make a sauce; pour over ham. Increase oven temperature to 400° F. and bake ½ hour longer, or until a meat thermometer registers about 150°. Baste frequently.

Boiled potatoes, creamed or plain spinach, and chilled white wine or a dry rosé or beer are fine accompaniments. I suppose, if you have the head for it, which I haven't, a mint julep would be all right too.

Speaking of beer, Marya once gave Norton an authentic British beer mug from an authentic British pub, and it is his treasure. Absolutely great for a refresher if he is doing hot, sweaty work in the garden on a hot summer day.

Speaking of rosé, I am not an addict as usually I find it too sweet, but Mrs. Ernest Hemingway, our Mary, once presented us with several bottles of Bourgogne, Rosé de Marsannay, 1967, which was dry and very good.

Not only does Mrs. H. give you nice presents when she is a guest, she entertains you in the grand manner when she is a hostess. We once had the pleasure of spending ten days with her in Ketchum, Idaho, a state with areas of majestic beauty which we had never before explored.

The house, in which her late husband, Ernest Hemingway wrote part of A Moveable Feast, and in which he died, overlooks Big Wood River and the Sawtooth Mountains, and while there are not many rooms, it is spacious and comfortable.

The day after our arrival, Mary needed the space. She gives an annual party on July 21, which was Ernest's birthday. This time there were to be eighty with the exception of ourselves all people who had known him. Meandering around on the terrace, along the deck or balcony flanking the house and below on the lawn there would have been ample room for everybody. But! It was one of the times of which I have already spoken. Not rain, but overcast skies and a chill wind blowing. At six thousand feet you sometimes get it.

Men came in the afternoon to string lights but said they would wait until evening before putting up the lanterns in case it might rain. When it became apparent that there was little likelihood of that they returned and finished the job and after holding a consultation with the caterers it was decided that while drinks might safely be served outdoors, it was too cold to eat out. The tables would have to be set up in the big living room.

We all set to work moving furniture, and the staff went into action. As the guests began arriving, Norton and I could only congratulate Mary on the efficiency and workability of the arrangements.

Like any intelligent person, Mrs. Hemingway is quick to respect those who, realizing they cannot cope with alcohol, have the guts and common sense to give it up entirely. Her view of those who eschew it for so-called moral reasons and who won't drink tea or coffee either because they might be "stimulants" is less sympathetic, although she considers it their own business. For people who don't drink themselves and who would try to impose their quirky prohibition on the rest of mankind, in short for the Carry Nations of the world she, and a legion of cohorts among whom I am happy to count myself, conjoin in a swift kick in the pants.

Since, by and large, Mary's friends and acquaintances are normal folk appreciating a sociable nip from time to time, her motto, especially at a party, is "Make the booze available." None of this business of guests sneaking into the pantry for a surreptitious nip.

There were two long bars, admirably stocked and manned. One was at the far end of the deck overlooking the mountains, one on the upper terrace, inevitably facing mountains too, and there the steel band was stationed. It was the most sympathetic steel band I ever heard for the simple reason that they played softly. They seemed gratified when I complimented them but added proudly that they also worked at the local night club, the Slavey, and could play *much* louder than that. "Please," I murmured, "stay as sweet as you are."

While the liquor may have flowed so did the food. I have rarely seen so impressive a pre-dinner smorgasbord. There was a long sideboard laden with a quite staggering assortment of victuals. Big, delicious, cold shrimp, equally delicious hot shrimp. Small sausages and bite-sized nubbins of succulent fried chicken.

There were platters of raw vegetables with an exceptionally good dip, a great block of pâté de foie gras, and a loaf of the best steak tartare I have ever eaten—ground, lean raw beef of high quality combined with raw egg, chopped anchovies, capers, chopped onion, and chives. Guests helped themselves, spreading it on small, thin slices of rye bread. There were tiny stuffed tomatoes and slices of salami and rounds of toast with subtle, mysterious spreads.

"Mary," I glurped, my mouth full, "this is madness. Who'll have room for dinner?"

Mary's glance was friendly but held an admixture of bafflement and surprise. "You ask people to dinner, for God's sake, you don't want them to starve." There was scant danger.

When we finally did move indoors to dine, the tables, while fairly closely ranked, were gay with bright red cloths and flowers. Although it is true that there was some food left over, the diminution of the roast beef, turkey with sweet and sour sauce, rice, salad of tomatoes, cucumber, pineapple, onions and green peppers followed by cheese and fruit, not to mention the contents of the wine bottles, was notable. That mountain air gives people good appetites.

Later in our stay Mary typed up the recipe for the turkey for me. She learned about the sauce from the chef of the Hotel Pacifico in Havana when she and Ernest Hemingway were living in Cuba.

As she said, she's a little vague on the amounts because the size of the turkey will obviously depend on the number of people who are going to eat it, but herewith the basics.

Turkey with Sweet-Sour Sauce

(Serves about 24)

10- to 12-pound turkey	Juice of 4 limes
2 Bermuda onions, quartered	2½ cups chicken broth
2 apples, peeled, cored, and	5 tablespoons cornstarch
quartered	2½ cups dry white wine
5 peaches	½ cup granulated sugar
¾ cup white grapes	⅓ cup white vinegar
1½ teaspoons fresh grated	1 tablespoon soy sauce
ginger root	Salt and pepper to taste

Stuff turkey with the onions and apples. Cook in plastic bag as directed on bag package label. When done, cool and remove meat from bones (about 16 cups turkey meat).

Meanwhile, gently stew fresh peaches and remove skins. Combine in bowl with grapes, grated ginger root, and lime juice. Marinate while turkey is roasting.

In a saucepan, blend a small amount of chicken broth into the cornstarch to make a smooth paste. Gradually add remaining broth and white wine. Simmer over low heat, stirring constantly, until mixture begins to thicken. Add remaining ingredients, and cook, stirring constantly, until mixture is thoroughly cooked. Drain juice from fruits; add fruit to sauce with the cooked turkey. Turn into baking dishes. Heat in 350° F. oven about 30 to 45 minutes, or until heated through. Serve with rice as an accompaniment.

After Mary Hemingway's party, we froze the small amount that was left over and ate it a few days later. It tasted even better the second time around, although that may have been because we had not already blunted our appetites on sumptuous hors d'oeuvre.

The leftover salad we ate the very next day for lunch. It was still unwilted, so Mary added a small amount of sugar, which, while not noticeable, blunted the somewhat sharp, vinegary taste; ran it through the blender; and metamorphosed it into a delicious gazpacho. We also had fresh brook trout coated with corn meal and fried by Dr. Brown. It was a good meal.

Earlier that same morning, since I was the first one up, I had gone downstairs to open the back door for the men who were coming to clear away the tables and chairs. I then started breakfast.

Out there in those Idaho mountains most people have electric stoves, and I am accustomed to gas. As I burned a sausage and spattered an egg and the teakettle steamed like a witch's caldron, I had a spasm of humility. Well, well, I thought, look who's writing a cookbook. I am not deft with eggs. I can never break the shells into two equal halves and I tend to put my thumb through the yolk. When separating whites and yolks I get the shakes and sometimes have to fish out a bit of yellow from the whites with a spoon. I have now, to some extent, remedied that by investing sixty-nine cents in an egg separator. What gives me courage to go on with this book is that this is not an official cookbook. It is a book with recipes in it. Ones that people will enjoy, I trust.

And there is one thing I have learned. Well, perhaps two things. The novice cook's great allies are the double boiler and asbestos mats. Fire is the Janus of the elements. Man's best friend and man's, or, more usually, in the domestic kitchen, woman's, greatest enemy. Too hot a flame can undo hours of meticulous labor. The double boiler and the asbestos mat keep the demon under control.

Another handy help is softened butter. If I am about to cook, Get Out the Butter is my first admonition to myself. If you have a cool place where it won't turn liquid, keep it there for a short time instead of in the refrigerator.

Also when cooking, keep the kettle going. A splash of boiling water can, in some instances, do you a world of good.

Sun Valley, the famed ski resort, is only about a mile from Ketchum and you'd be surprised how many people, living in Ketchum, but who can have their choice, claim Sun Valley as their address. They think it has a grander sound.

Mary drove us to the Lodge, which, as everyone knows, is chockablock with skiers in winter but far from deserted during the summer. We also drove around the environs and the experience was a saddening one. Where there used to be open meadows and the uplands blending into the foothills and mountains, there are now great spreading scabs of campers' automobiles and mobile homes. Relentlessly vulgar, relentlessly ugly.

Dedicated efforts are being made to arrest the cancerous growth, one of the most intelligent, well-balanced and farseeing warriors being Mollee Hecht, who runs the Ketchum book shop, but much of the desecration is already a *fait accompli* and cannot be changed. They have got so far as to pass a law decreeing that when the horrible glaring tin that roofs many of the houses begins to disintegrate, it must be painted a neutral tone or replaced with a less blinding substance, but in the meantime it is eye-shattering and offensive.

Naturally there are exceptions: houses that are well planned and architecturally distinguished, but much of the new growth makes one despair not only of the national taste but of the national common sense.

There are all kinds of complexes and condominiums of dark, troglodyte, inexpressibly dreary houses huddled together so as to insure no privacy at all. The expensive ones look like the barracks of a reformatory. The cheap ones are like privies sticking up on the landscape.

Possibly some day some one will plant a tree or flower but that moment of revelation is not yet upon us. Everything is built smack on the main roads, but for that, at least, there is reason. The snow lies deep for many months of the year and plowing out a driveway is difficult and costly.

By way of a change one pleasing local sight is the memorial erected to Ernest Hemingway by the residents of Ketchum who had been his friends. A simple shaft topped by a bronze head set among trees beside a swiftly running brook.

The other nice place is the skating rink at the Lodge which is kept frozen through the summer. Saturday nights they serve a buffet dinner and afterward there is an ice-skating exhibition. A few of their performers may be well-known names although mostly they are kids and aspirants who come from all over the country, but even those who were not Olympic contenders looked good to me, darting like swallows and swifter than the wind.

A less athletic evening we spent with Clara Spiegel, a good friend of Mary Hemingway's, not to mention the rest of her acquaintances, for Mrs. Spiegel cooks! And when Mrs. Spiegel cooks, the guests eat.

Her small individual filet steaks were excellent, but the unexpected pleasure—it's always nice if you can serve at least one "Oh, what's this?" dish—was cold Iranian cucumber soup.

When I asked Clara where she got it and she told me, it touched a chord other than vocal. Clara had known Peggy Harvey. Peggy is dead now, but she was a friend of ours, and she wrote cookbooks, the best-known of which were *When the Cook's Away, Season to Taste,* and *The Horn of Plenty.*

Peggy was an attractive woman. In her youth she had been a model and she never lost her model's figure no matter how much or what she ate. Some of her friends didn't like her for that. Looking at her and knowing her culinary skills and opportunities, they muttered dark imprecations. "She is a witch." "There is no God."

Since Clara Spiegel has a pretty neat figure herself, not to mention Mrs. Hemingway, who is as small and slim-hipped as they come, neither of them ever felt that way about Peggy. It was Clara who brought her and Mary together and it was through Peggy that Norton and I originally met Mary. We toasted her memory in the delicious soup which she had brought into our lives.

Cold Iranian Cucumber Soup

(Serves 4–6)

3 cups yogurt	3 tablespoons minced chives
1½ cups grated cucumber	½ teaspoon salt
½ cup seedless raisins	½ teaspoon white pepper
¾ inch cold water	2 chopped hard-cooked eggs
1 tablespoon minced fresh dill *or*	(optional)
¼ teaspoon dried	

Beat yogurt in an electric mixer. Add cucumber and raisins. Blend and add cold water. Blend and add dill, chives, salt, and white pepper. Blend well. Chill at least two hours, or it can be made early and chilled all day. If it is to be the mainstay of the meal, add the chopped eggs.

Along with the recipe, Mrs. Spiegel handed me a lighthearted limerick, a little composition of her own, which I herewith append, but probably a more practical accompaniment would be the Norwegian flatbread available at many of the better grocery stores and greatly savored at her table.

> There once was a chef in Iran
> Whose cucumber measured three span
> His concubines moaned
> With delight to be owned
> By this fine Persian version of man

Norwegian Flatbread

2 sections of flatbread per person	Well-softened butter
	Celery Salt

Butter the flatbread evenly and thinly. Sprinkle with the salt. Place on a cookie sheet and warm in a low oven until the butter has melted and absorbed the salt. Serve hot.

The day after Clara Spiegel's party we started out for our trip on the Salmon River. The best fun of travel always seems to be the little trips within the parent trip.

When Norton and I first went around the world, our five-day cruise through the Greek islands was one of the memorable interludes of our lives. Another was when we were visiting our friends the Astley Bells in Djakarta and flew for a few days to Bali.* When we were in Fiji we went on an enchanted cruise aboard a little ship The Stardust.† And, when in Katmandu, we went overnight to Tiger Tops.‡

The diversion Mary had arranged involved driving some 250 miles to a place called Corn Creek, where we would pick up a boat and a river pilot.

The first days drive would bring us to the little town of Salmon, and it was decided that the six of us in two cars would rendezvous for a picnic lunch en route.

* The Carthaginian Rose
† Second Spring and Two Potatoes
‡ Around the World and Other Places

Our party consisted of our hostess, Mollee Hecht, the conservationist and fighter for the defense of the earth; her son John, recently sprung from a three-year stint in the Navy; and an engaging creature, Gioia Larkin, a notably young-looking mother of six; Norton; and me.

We considered ourselves a reasonably worldly and sophisticated group and we turned out to be just as dopey as everybody else in our choice of a picnic spot.

We came upon a very pretty one. Off the main road on the other side of the river along a shady path. We all opted for that, but when she saw a fisherman poised on a nearby rock Mary decided no, we might disturb him or he us and we would be better elsewhere.

Our little caravan set off again. We drove and we drove and we drove. Finally, tired, cranky, and hungry we just plain stopped on the road, let down the tail gate of the jeep, and ate our lunch in the hot sun and full view of every passing car. The lunch was good so our equanimity was quickly restored although subsequently shaken when Gioia returned from having deposited a bag of trash in a place indicated for the purpose and said mildly, "I thought you'd like to know that just around the bend there's a lovely shady spot with picnic tables set up and not a soul in sight."

The following day, driving the seventy miles along a narrow winding road bordering the Salmon River, which is by the way a fair piece of stream, being four hundred and twenty-five miles long, Mary inveighed against the number of cars we passed. "Two years ago when I made this trip there wasn't *one*. Now look! We must have passed at least six."

For those accustomed to the highways of the east, six seems modest, but fundamentally she was right. In another two years, twenty or thirty. In five or six years bumper to bumper. And yet there is a glimmer of light. In New York at least the birth rate is falling. In New Jersey many obstetricians are concentrating exclusively on gynecology, and gynecologists are not happy.

Business is perhaps less good for the Pamper people and the

manufacturers of baby food but the earth itself is getting a breather.

However, even the most optimistic estimates foresee seventy years before the ideal population growth, zero, is attained. And that is only maybe.

Having survived the offending six cars, we arrived at Corn Creek and met Bob Smith, the river pilot, and his young wife Jill. Jill was about five months pregnant with their second child. Once we started on the river it occurred to me, that were a woman so minded the trip might well substitute for a hospital abortion. It would have to be a tenacious embryo that survived. That river ride is rugged.

We were in a big, open, flat-bottom boat with two powerful outboard jet motors kicking us along at tremendous speed. All that part of the river is fairly wide with hills and mountains and marching pines rising on either side. The Salmon River Gorge is the second deepest on the continent. A fifth of a mile deeper than the Grand Canyon and surpassed only by the Snake River Canyon. There are a few quiet stretches and pools of dark water, but mostly the river races and eddies around rocks visible and gushes and gurgles and drops over rocks invisible yet well known, one can only hope, to the pilot, and hurls itself in what I suppose are low rapids, three to four feet, from a higher level to a lower, where the swirling water is very white indeed and where one has the impression that were the boat to swerve an inch to the right or left it would bash against a boulder and one would be quite dead quite soon. As a government brochure states with simple candor, "The amateur should remember that chances of rescue in case of upset are poor." Poor? I should think nonexistent. An impression heightened by the fact that that stretch is known as the River of No Return.

As things stand now, one must return or else continue on into the Snake River, which flows into the Columbia which eventually empties into the Pacific.

In the early days when the vast tract of country was being opened up that's exactly what travelers had to do, since before motors it was impossible to get back up the river against the current and there were no roads. Also there were the Nez Percé and the Shoshone Indians to contend with.

In its normal course, every time the prow of our boat rose into the air it would come smashing down on what, despite one's senses telling one was water, had to be concrete. Crash, bang, clatter, crash and drenching spray. Exhilarating! Counting going and coming we would be doing 180 miles of it.

Apparently when Mary had made the trip two years previously, she and Bob had had the river pretty much to themselves. Today one passes raft after rubber raft loaded with trippers. To us they all looked too crowded for comfort, but with fewer passengers traveling at a much slower pace and without the noise of an engine other than a small auxiliary to be used occasionally on the return trip upstream, the experience, I would imagine, might be very pleasant.

As it was we had a great deal. Magnificent scenery, a skillful navigator, and cheery companionship. The only disappointment was the lack of wildlife.

We did see briefly a moose and a family of handsome mountain goats: Pa, Ma, and Baby, a lovely fawn color and splendid horns and they appeared as sure-footed as they are reputed to be, but there were virtually no birds. Gioia claimed to have seen a small bear earlier on but before she could call attention to him he had vanished.

Gioia and her husband Chuck Larkin have a ranch thirty or forty miles from Ketchum and breed beef cattle. She has a family of dogs and also a coyote whom she dearly loves, and that endeared her to me, as I think they are fine animals. I have small use for the sheep men's wearisome, old-hat "goldarn varmint" attitude and all that bounty business and the unspeakable cruelty of the way animals are killed. One can only hope that those who perpetrate these atrocities will meet with equally agonizing deeds.

Mr. and Mrs. Larkin have another pet, however, a somewhat unorthodox dependent: a boa constrictor called, logically enough, B.C. When Gioia told me about him, *my* flesh also crawled.

B.C. lives in the house. I believe he is confined to his own quarters, should they have any fainthearted guests, but when the family travels back and forth from the ranch to their house in Scottsdale, Arizona, B.C. goes along in the car just like everybody else. Must come as quite a surprise to the gas-station men.

Above the motors and the banging and the spray, Gioia shouted out bits of information about him until it was time for lunch, when we came ashore at a sort of deserted lodge that Jill and Bob rent from the government, which apparently keeps an avuncular eye on its maintenance. We had some of our own food left over from the picnic the day before and packed in one of those containers that holds ice for twenty-four hours or so and keeps things fresh; but also, young Jill proved a fine provider. She brought forth cold fried chicken and an excellent salad.

Jill's Salad

(Serves 8–10)

1 can (approximately 1 pound) kidney beans, drained

1 can (approximately 20 ounces) chick-peas, drained

1 can (one pound) cut green beans, drained

1 can (15 ounces) butter beans, drained

¼ cup finely minced onion

French dressing

In large bowl, combine all vegetables. Add enough French dressing to marinate. Chill and let flavors blend several hours or overnight.

The virtues of this dish are fourfold. It is delicious, it is nourishing, it is easy to prepare, it is inexpensive. And to my way of thinking infinitely preferable to those all-time American favorites, tuna fish and hot dogs. In telling a friend of mine about it I happened to observe that Norton had particularly enjoyed it. "I bet he did," she said, "men don't like just lettuce leaves. They like salads with *things* in them." That's been my experience too.

About four or five in the afternoon we came to Crooked Creek and the Shepp Ranch, where we would be staying for a couple of nights. The ranch is primitive but nice, and familiarity is the word. The minute you are introduced everybody calls you by your first name.

I know the custom is not only western. Today if you say to Dotty Delphinium, "I'd like you to meet Cassandra Mendle-coop," even though they have never clapped eyes on each other before they say, "Hello, Dotty," "Hello, Cassandra."

With young people of the same age it's understandable. Anything else would seem stilted. And on the few occasions when I may be recognized from a television appearance, it sounds perfectly natural if people on the street sing out, "Hello, Ilka."

When I am introduced in a drawing room, as Ilka Chase or Ilka Brown and the other person says, "Hello, Ilka," although I know it is today's coinage, I can't help it, I still get a slight shock.

A friend a generation behind me says she likes it. Especially when younger people do it. "It shows they don't consider me old."

Maybe. But the fact is if they are very young I *am* older than they are. If the use of one's last name seems unbearably square, a courteous "How do you do" shouldn't be too difficult. However there is another reason why a little restraint—perhaps an hour or so—seems desirable. I do not warm to instant familiarity.

I dare say I date back to the wimple, but I enjoy leisurely progression, intimacy by stages. I think it's nice to have some place to go in an acquaintanceship.

Where an instant first-name basis is inevitable and natural is in the entertainment world because there, even though people may not have come face to face before, they know each other by sight and reputation. A freemasonry prevails. Yet even in show biz I would consider it inappropriate for a young bit player to address, shall we say, Lord Olivier with a "Hi ya, Larry." I bet the Lord would too.

Meanwhile, back at the ranch . . . the bunkhouse consisted of two big rooms, each with three double-decker beds. Norton and young John Hecht had one room and Mary, Gioia, Mollee, and I returned to boarding school and shared the other. When Norton and I met outside to kiss good night, I felt as though any minute Miss Parks, the mathematics teacher, would come and catch us. It was Miss Parks who always used to catch us at midnight feasts.

My memory of those far-distant repasts is that they consisted largely of marshmallow whip and pickles, although surely we must have done better than that. Probably what I am really remembering is the indigestion invoked by them.

The ranch was run by Mr. and Mrs. Schubert. Mrs. Hemingway, being of a cultural background remembered their name by thinking of the famed composer. I thought of Lee and Jake.

The food they served was simple but good, delicious buckwheat cakes for breakfast, and the Schuberts are not likely to run out of the wherewithal for cooking them or anything else. The kitchen is equipped with an electric stove, a gas stove, and a coal stove. Let it rain, let it blow, let it snow.

The following day we went for a much more leisurely trip on the river, since we didn't have to get anywhere at any time, and it was most enjoyable. Norton and Gioia fished for trout, and the rest of us went swimming. There are any number of pretty little sandy beaches or bars as the local people call them. To say that I went swimming is more a figure of speech since even off our own beach on a hot August day I laze about in the water rather than swim. The water of the Salmon River, despite glorious sunshine, must have registered all of three degrees, and all I did was dip, gasp, and clamber out, my lips quite blue. Mollie, John, and Mary cavorted with the fortitude of the salmon themselves.

Our fishermen returned with enough trout to make an ample luncheon, but Bob cooked them over the fire on sliced onion and wrapped in foil. Foil is my idea of pure hell except when used as a cover to keep something warm while a sauce or other accompaniment is being prepared.

Potatoes baked in it are a disaster; soggy on the outside, raw within, and while I certainly disposed of my portion I couldn't help but wish Bob had followed Mummy's example in the old nursery rhyme.

> Little fishy in a brook,
> Daddy caught him on a hook,
> Mummy fried him in a pan,
> Baby ate him like a man.

The next day we returned back up the river. Heaving ourselves over the rapids going upstream was, oddly enough, not as arduous as dropping down. Less spine-cracking.

In Salmon we returned to the Herndon Motel for the night, and at breakfast the next morning I was amused to see the number of men who sat at table wearing their Stetson hats and speaking with a western drawl in the best movie tradition.

The hats at table took me back to my girlhood. On the rare occasions when my mother left her office at *Vogue* to lunch at home with a few friends she and her guests all wore their hats throughout the meal.

The night we returned to Ketchum we dined with Ernest Hemingway's son Jack and Puck, his wife. On the lawn in the lovely light of evening their youngest daughter, a kid of about eight, was turning handsprings and frolicking with four golden retrievers.

We had delicious charcoal-broiled chicken, and with cocktails Puck served a kind of ceviche made with mountain trout. Ceviche is a grand first course, and those who cannot obtain trout need not feel deprived if they use the following recipe.

I first came upon it several years ago when Mrs. Bartley Crumm was running an original and extremely helpful service called Menus by Mail. You subscribed to it and at regular intervals received a kind of news letter of menus and recipes. This is the one for ceviche.

Ceviche

(Serves 6)

1 pound fillet of sole, flounder, or halibut (sole and halibut are more delicate)

1 cup lemon or lime juice (or enough to cover fish as it marinates)

2 tomatoes, peeled, seeded, and cut into small pieces

1½ teaspoons finely minced onion

2 teaspoon salt

6 tablespoons olive oil

¼ teaspoon powdered thyme

1 teaspoon powdered bay leaf (this is hard to find, so you may have to use 1 small bay leaf, crushed very fine)

2 tablespoons oregano flakes *or* 1 tablespoon fresh oregano

12 drops Tabasco sauce

⅓ cup finely minced parsley

Cut the fish into small, bite-size pieces and marinate in the lemon or lime juice in a covered bowl in the refrigerator overnight or for several hours.

Combine the tomatoes, minced onion, and salt in a small bowl. Although Mrs. Crumm's recipe doesn't call for it, a little finely chopped avocado is also pleasant. In another bowl mix the remaining ingredients except the parsley. About 2 hours before serving, drain fish, wash under running water, and pat dry with paper towel. Mix fish with all the other ingredients and stir in the parsley. This should be served very cold in small bowls or scallop shells, the kind used for Coquille St. Jacques. Clara Spiegel's Norwegian flatbread would be a nice accompaniment.

This is a delicious first course or may be served with cocktails before going to the table as Mrs. Jack Hemingway did it.

Since we were feasting so much in the evenings our lunches at home tended to be simple and one day Mary dished up a good quick one, ideal for hot weather. It was a shrimp salad. Since there aren't many shrimps handy in the Sawtooth Mountains these were frozen but they tasted fine.

Mary Hemingway's Easy Shrimp Salad

(Serves 4 abundantly)

Two one-pound packages of ready-to-serve frozen shrimp. Half a can of chick-peas. Sliced scallions, finely chopped green pepper, and two or three finely chopped stalks of celery. This was served with a dressing of store mayonnaise spiked with olive oil, lime juice, salt and pepper. With it we ate hot tortillas, and it was a good and satisfying meal.

We had two fine summer desserts while we were in Ketchum, both simple and both delicious. We dined one evening with Dr. and Mrs. John Moritz and Mary Ellen served this.

Wine Jelly

(Serves 4–6)

1½ envelopes (1½ tablespoons) unflavored gelatin
½ cup cold water
1 cup boiling water

2 tablespoons lemon juice
1 cup granulated sugar
1 cup sherry
2 tablespoons brandy
Heavy cream

Soften gelatin in the cold water; add boiling water and stir until gelatin is dissolved. Blend in the lemon juice, sugar, sherry, and brandy. Pour into bowl or individual dishes; refrigerate until jelled. Serve with whipped cream.

It's Jell-O, but what Jell-O! A rich amber color and a rich amber taste.

The other good dessert was presented to us at Mollee Hecht's house when we dined with her our last night in Ketchum. This too is easily prepared and oh so good.

Mollee Hecht's Specialty

(Serves 6–8)

1 package (8 ounces) cream cheese, softened	1 cup heavy cream
	1 cup white seedless grapes
1 cup sour cream	1 cup chopped pecans

Blend together until a soft, creamy consistency the cream cheese, sour cream, and heavy cream. Then fold in the white grapes and chopped pecans. Cool, pretty, and delicious.

Another dessert involving white grapes was given to me by an old friend and a notable collector of cookbooks, Madelin Gilpatrick. Easy and excellent.

Dessert

White grapes	Cointreau
Litchi nuts	Lemon
Kirsch	

All you do is toss together white grapes and canned or fresh litchi nuts—if fresh, remove the pits—kirsch, and a little bit of Cointreau, just enough to give a trace of orange flavor. Sprinkle with grated lemon peel. Serve cold. Amounts depend on the number of people to be served.

Since Mary Hemingway did so much to make our visit memorable and enjoyable I like to think we comported ourselves acceptably. Still, no matter how special, a house is a house, a locale we are accustomed to. Life on the deep is something else again and landlubbers may need a little guidance if invited for a seagoing weekend.

I hope I may be forgiven for yacht dropping but I have been on a few deluxe craft in my day, among them the *Christina*. This may come as a surprise to Mrs. Aristotle Onassis, but it was in 1956. I was writing a syndicated newspaper column and I had gone to Monaco at the time of the Grace Kelly-Prince Rainier wedding.*

Mr. Onassis and his previous missus were hospitable to the press, and we frequently streamed like lemmings up and down the gangplank and wined and dined on board feeling very grand to be in such sumptuous surroundings.

As a result of these occasional flights above my station, I should say that if a yacht is large, built for pleasure and there is a crew, with the exception of fishing and perhaps swimming over the side, the routine and protocol are not all that different from life ashore. It's on small boats that one must be wary.

When the aforementioned Mrs. Anderson, she who wished to moan alone after a guest-filled weekend, was married to Mr. Anderson, much of their time was spent at sea. Mr. A. was a Vasco Da Gama type and a notable navigator. Nor was his bride averse to water. She once won the commodore's award for the greatest progress made that season by a neophyte, but in the course of cruising a sliver or two of iron did enter her soul.

What caused it was the fact that at that period she had in her employ the dream couple of the world. The woman was an incomparable cook, the man the perfect butler. Under the circumstances, Mrs. Anderson had visions of herself in a ruffled gown on a chaise longue, stroking a toy poodle, reading high-class pornography and nibbling sweetmeats.

That wasn't quite how things worked out. It was the couple who nibbled and lolled at home while the madam spent most of her time in the ship's galley cooking for her husband and their friends.

She told me she got to be very chummy with the gimbals, adding, "The trouble is you're not set in a gimbal, only the burners. One brisk heave and you can go skittering across the galley and out the door."

Other aspects of the seafaring life irked her as well. They were news to me and I mention two or three of them so if you are in-

* *The Carthaginian Rose*

vited to spend a couple of days aboard a small boat they won't give you the heave ho.

The first thing is luggage. Don't take big, square, rigid pieces. There is no place to stow them. Take duffle bags or something of the sort. Anything that is flexible and can be squashed without being harmed.

If you want to take a boat present, that is praiseworthy, but don't make it a large ham or a big birthday cake or a watermelon. The ice chest can't accommodate them.

If you take a bottle or two, well and good, but don't leave bottles or glasses setting casually on a table. They will slide off. Set them in the racks provided.

The minute you're up in the morning, fold away your bedding. Where you slept is where you and others on board will sit.

Another pointer, and herewith the cardinal sin, do *not* repeat *not* smear yourself with grease or sun-tan oil. This wreaks havoc with a teakwood deck. The damn stuff never comes off.

Furthermore, watch your heels. Sharp, pointed spikes are not in fashion at the moment but if they ever come back do not wear them when boarding a friend's yacht. They too destroy the deck.

Also in the vicinity of the compass don't equip yourself like a hardware store with metal lighters, pen knives, watch bracelets, or whatever. They get the compass confused.

Ruth Anderson told me of a time when her husband was nearly driven up the rigging. Mr. Anderson had just had his compass boxed. I do not understand about this but old salts will. All was perfection. They had invited on board a friend, a professional navy man and full commander. As he stood behind his host the compass needle began swinging madly. They were off course to the north, off course to the south, they were twirling in wild circles. Mr. Anderson's blood pressure was rising, Mrs. Anderson's stomach was gently heaving, and then the cause of the confusion was located. For reasons of his own the splendid representative of the United States mighty naval force was wearing a compass on his hat. When you are invited out for a sail don't do that.

CHAPTER NINE

The Lost Art

The lost art, once as flourishing as the painting and sculpture of the Renaissance, as the literature and commerce of the Elizabethans, is of course that of correspondence. How rarely do we write letters today. Indeed how old-fashioned has a telegram become!

Business correspondence to some extent is still in force although teletype communication is supplanting it, and families and friends separated by great distances, if they don't have big incomes, may still write occasionally. If they're rich they telephone. As the ads of the telephone company remind us, short of the loved one's touch the sound of the loved one's voice imparts the most immediate impact.

I don't knock it. Instant communication is a marvelous blessing, but a letter can be very endearing. For separated lovers, I'm not sure a letter isn't even better than a phone call. It is something to hold and to cherish. To read over and over again, and it is *personal.* Handwriting is as self-revealing as a voice, as a footstep.

I once knew a girl who had been very cozy with two tap dancers. After all, we consort with the people we meet and in her theatrical field she met tap dancers. Both gentlemen were Big Names and both had recorded their skill. Without looking at the labels, and may I be struck by lightning if this isn't true, when she listened to their albums she knew which was which.

But the secret of good correspondence, as anyone experienced in the art of separation will tell you, is to write frequently. Daily if possible. The more you do it the easier it is.

The hurdle and the boring part is to sit down after many a moon and start off. Dear Alfredo. Dear Clementine. *Now* what am I going to say? When the chasm is too wide and deep, bridge building scarcely seems worth while. But when two people know the details of each other's life, letters can become like a fascinating story. Did the gas-station man finally sell his business, and to whom? Did old Mrs. Summers win the lawsuit against that pig who was claiming a nonexistent right of way across her property? Is Mimi's baby born yet? Girl or boy? And of course the excitement of the big deal. What *is* Alex's situation? Chairman of the board or president of the company? Jennifer got the part in the Broadway show! You bought the house? How great!

During every war, letters to and from men fighting far from home are vital links in helping to hang onto sanity in the midst of madness.

My husband, although at that time we were not married, served on a carrier in the Pacific in World War Two. He was away for sixteen months, and I wrote him nearly every day and he wrote me almost as often and amid all the horror I will say for the United States mails that they *did* get through. We numbered our letters and not one was missing.

I should not care to embark on World War Three in order to achieve it, but it would be nice if someone would come up with a plan to improve our peacetime postal service which is, shall we say, less than arrow-swift.

Certain letters we are obligated to write and let us hope we do not find the task too irksome. Bread-and-butter letters should always be sent, although common sense can apply there as well as in other departments of life. If you've had a rare visit write a rare letter but if good friends are frequent weekend visitors in each other's houses wild outpourings of gratitude would hardly seem necessary. A telephone call or a comment about how much fun we had the next time we meet should suffice.

If, however, we are staying with friends who take us to dine with other friends of theirs, a little note to the unfamiliar hostess is a courteous gesture.

Letters of condolence should never be neglected. They can mean a great deal to one who has been bereaved. If you are moved to write an appreciative letter to an artist in any field, obey that impulse! The actor, the painter, the writer *enjoys* it.

Sometimes, sitting alone day after day working on a book an author thinks, What am I doing this for? Is anyone on earth going to read it?

If he has pulled a booboo he will discover in short order that he has a reading public hitherto undreamed of! Four out of every five people in the United States will write in to tell him he is an unmitigated ass. Not to mention Europeans who have caught him in translation. A larger number, by the way, than many authors would suspect from glancing at their royalty statements. The infrequent words of praise do something to heal the scars and are cherished.

Write also to your congressmen and senators. Let them hear the voice of the people! That's what they're there for.

If you are traveling don't be chary of sending letters and postcards. You may make your friends envious but it warms the recipient's hearts to know that even in the midst of foreign sights and sounds you are thinking of them.

And let stay-at-homes write to travelers! No matter if they *are* having Wonderful Time, the first act of everyone arriving at a new hotel is a dash to the desk to inquire if there are letters from home.

And speaking of traveling, there are two moments when friends can mean a great deal to each other. When they leave and when they come home. People who have families—parents, children, sisters, brothers—are less vulnerable at such times because almost automatically the family is there to say good-by and to welcome them back.

A solitary voyager does not have this to rely on and is therefore doubly appreciative when friends are at hand. It is nice when someone waves you a fond and encouraging farewell even when you have the stimulation and excitement of the trip to look forward to. When you come home it makes a world of difference if a friend or friends are there to greet you. It is sorrowful to have to arrive unmet at an airport or dock or bus terminal, wherever it may be that marks the journey's end. There is a break in the continuity of one's life. Friendship creates a sort of happy bridging of the time away back into one's normal routine.

CHAPTER TEN

Friends in the Hospital

Even the stanchest spirit is likely to succumb, if only temporarily, to self-pity and the mopes when incarcerated in a hospital because of illness or an operation. It is a time for chums to rally, to spread a little cheer.

But tread warily. If one is under the weather few interludes are more exhausting than those one must submit to when an extrovert pal barges in, jollity at the ready, strewing bonhomie like a demented sower of grain.

The ill tire easily. Even when everything is mending nicely convalescence may be prolonged and invalids have no out. They can't very well say, "I hate shooing you off but I must run, I'm late for an appointment." Or "Do forgive me, dear, but we're having a couple of business pals of Harry's and I have to get dinner started." Or "I've got to pick up the twins at school." Hapless invalids haven't "got to" anything. There they are and there they're stuck. Be merciful.

Let us suppose a member of the family or a friend has had an operation. The most thoughtful thing we can do the first day or two is to send flowers, call up and inquire of the nurse how things are going, and ask her to extend our love and wishes for a speedy recovery. But apropos of flowers, if an operation has been serious, hold them in reserve. A patient sometimes remains in the recovery room two or three days or, even if back in his own bed, may be too ill to take in his surroundings. Wait a bit, see how the land lies, before tossing the bouquets.

I do not like to strike a morbid note but inevitably if one thinks of hospitals and serious illness by a natural sequence one is brought to a contemplation of death. When I think of funeral flowers I always think of my old friend Charles Brackett, who wrote so many of Hollywood's brighter comedies.

Charles is dead now, but he had been devoted to my mother, and when he read of her death in the paper he phoned me immediately from the coast asking where the funeral was to be as he wanted to send flowers. I thanked him but said, "It isn't really necessary Charlie. There were one or two charities Mother was interested in, maybe you'd rather send them a contribution." Charlie's voice cracked like a whip across twenty-five hundred miles of the mighty mountains and the fertile plains. "No, Ilka! I'll be goddamned if I want Edna to be a tax deduction." Nor was she.

To think of Charles is to think of Elizabeth, his longtime wife, and of their Hollywood parties. They gave some of the nicest in their charming house in Bel Air.

One that I recall was for me. I had returned to Hollywood to do some job or other and Charles and Elizabeth asked me to dine. I sat on Charles's right, and on my right was a man who seemed amiable enough but who didn't strike me as having a great deal of personality, and truth to tell I didn't pay much attention to him.

Afterward, as we left the table, I muttered to Charles, "Who was that fella next to me anyhow?"

My host sighed. "Dear Chasie, we try to do our little best for you. That fella was Jack Webb, only the biggest name in the entertainment business at the present time." It was indeed the hero of "Dragnet." "The facts, ma'am. Just the facts."

The Brackett food was always good, and one of Elizabeth's

specialties I have treasured. Strips of baked potato skin served with cocktails. It sounds odd, I know, but just try it.

Potato Skin Hors d'Oeuvre

(Serves 6)

| 3 medium-sized baking potatoes | Coarse salt |
| Melted butter | Freshly ground pepper |

Preheat oven to 375° F. Take the raw baking potatoes and with a very sharp knife remove the skin with a little potato adhering to it. What you want is strips about ¾ inch wide and 4 inches long. You should get about 26 pieces. Brush these with melted butter. Place on baking sheet or on foil laid on the baking sheet; bake 10 minutes.

Remove; drain on brown paper, sprinkle with coarse salt and the freshly ground black pepper; serve warm. They look well served on wooden plates or a wooden platter.

Use the potatoes themselves for dinner or puréed for Vichyssoise or cubed for some versions of New England clam chowder at another meal.

Everybody loves the crisp peel and you have the satisfaction of knowing they're wholesome and nourishing. No weird concoctions that conceivably could send you or a guest hightailing it to the hospital as some nut and shellfish dishes have been known to do.

Reverting to our invalids, I do not deny that there are some amusing Get Well cards on the market, but to a lesser degree, I feel about those the way I feel about commercial Condolence cards. The latter are inadmissible. Totally and always. If you don't care enough to write a letter don't communicate at all. The Get Wells, if they accompany flowers or a little present may skin by, but a personal note is like the touch of a hand. However, like the early visit, make the note short. When one is enfeebled, *pages* of writing take away the appetite like too large a helping on a plate.

A bright ray for those on the outside is when the patient is able to answer the phone himself and engage in a brief chat. Depending of course on the patient. It *may* be brief or we may be in for a fairly detailed replay of the proceedings in which event a true friend listens with sympathy and patience. The first time round. And at this stage of the game he must never never interrupt to tell the escapee from the valley of the shadow about *his* operation.

If visits are in order, hooray, but take it easy. No ailing person wants to be confronted by gloom and long tales of woe but neither are raucous laughter and the booming voice endearing.

I think everyone, grown women *and* men as well as children appreciate a little present when they are laid up. It brightens the long, tedious day.

And although a great many hospital rooms have television sets they do not, as a rule, have radios. A gift or a loan of one can make a big difference. If a person is sharing a semi-private room or is on a ward an earplug attachment is mandatory. And books are still the great lifesavers. I would ask only that we apply a little thought to their content. If someone has just had his leg amputated, don't give him a copy of *Moby Dick*.

If a dear one has had an appendectomy don't bring along the most hilarious novel of the decade or arrange for a private screening of a Woody Allen picture. If you've just had your appendix out and start laughing it's like a flaming sword thrust through your vitals.

I have found that if a friend speaks a foreign language one or two magazines of that country or those from Great Britain are greatly appreciated.

I remember an occasion when two or three of us got together and made up a crossword puzzle for a friend, using names, and places, and words that had special significance for him. It was a smash hit.

Eau de cologne is a light, refreshing thought. For a child a small aquarium is a happy diversion. There's nothing the matter with it for a grownup either, if the hospital stay is to be protracted.

I assume, wrongly I shouldn't be surprised, that everyone uses an eye shade, those masklife affairs with ribbon or elastic loops that slip over the ears and which are indispensable for keeping out light. If you have an ill friend who doesn't have one, procure it for him. Your name will be blessed forever.

Since most hospital food is really nothing you want to talk about, let alone eat, the simplest dish, if it is well prepared, is a heavenly relief.

I remember that once when I was in the hospital, Barbara Ziegler brought me a thick lamb chop. She had broiled it at home, wrapped it in foil and come full tilt in a taxicab. The chop was still hot and absolutely delectable.

Shortly after I had written about this Good Samaritan act, she and her husband Jimmy were visiting us in the country. "I'll never forget it," I said, "it's still the best chop I ever ate."

My friend looked puzzled. "Did I bring you a lamb chop?"

"You sure did."

"Funny. I remember I brought you some soup, but I'm afraid of lamb chops. I cook them, of course, but they always worry me to death. I never know how to tell when they're ready."

Possibly my memory played me a trick but I shall always associate Barbara with that succulent chop.

Diet permitting, a little booze is never turned down and a glass of wine with a hospital dinner may delude one into finding it quite palatable.

Because of the appalling cost and the pressing need for beds, patients are frequently dismissed when, although they may be completely out of danger, they are still in an enfeebled condition.

In those circumstances a truly princely gesture, if one can afford it, is an offer to pay a part-time cleaning woman or cook to come in for a couple of weeks to help out until the invalid is a little steadier on his pins.

But the most important thing of all is keeping in touch, letting ill friends know that we are thinking of them, that they are not forgotten.

Should you have loved ones in prison the same treatment probably applies.

Nor is this merely a quip. Given President Nixon's appointments to the Supreme Court and the actions of these gentlemen, harassing television networks, jailing reputable and dependable newspaper men who refuse to reveal their sources of information and who may print matter at odds with the judge's or governmental point of view, any number of the respectable can find themselves sojourning in the pokey.

CHAPTER ELEVEN

Cooks and Hostesses I Have Known
and Outputs I Have Eaten

I have had a great many cooks in the course of my life. I am experienced. Some people have had the same cook for years and years. They are lucky. I think an employer has the right to exact certain standards from an employee but I should not like to be considered mean or unfair.

Some of the changes have come about because of my moving from one place to another. Two demoiselles left to get married. Neither marriage, alas, came off but they were full of optimism. Another one died. One retired. Two were chronic drunks and got fired. So it went and so it goes. Scarcely a tale to hold children from play and old men from the chimney corner but an experience common to many.

The thing to keep telling yourself if you are on the changing circuit is that you are being enriched by these ever recurring new contacts. During the periods, these days more and more frequent, when the cook in your house is likely to be the face that greets you in the mirror in the morning, think of all you are learning.

Yet in one respect I am lucky. I have a husband who, when he puts his mind to it, can turn out a tasty dish. Of course he has his own preferences. I sometimes have to persuade him that, delicious and nutritious as broccoli and Brussels sprouts can be, eating them every night for a week on end gets a mite tedious.

Also we have a slight difference of opinion about breakfast. He wants coffee, a good substantial meal and a negligible lunch. I am not merely a coffee and juice person, I take tea, and I will go as far as an egg, but I cannot cope with the kind of morning fare so fancied by Australians. Juice, porridge, eggs, ham, steak, and toast.

What I like is a reasonably nourishing luncheon. Since my husband's normal fare is a sandwich at his desk around one-thirty, he is irked if, on weekends, he is asked to sit down at table, taking time away from his work around the place.

In his defense, however, I will say that his breakfast tastes are not quite so formidable as the Australians'. Three of his offerings that even I have little difficulty in demolishing are creamed finnan haddie, codfish cakes, and pancakes. Not all at the same meal.

He also makes an awfully good New England clam chowder, and to prove that he scatters his patronage impartially between fishmonger and butcher, an excellent butterfly lamb.

This is what he says about his recipes.

Creamed Finnan Haddie

(Serves 2 generously)

Smoked fillet of haddock	White pepper
Milk	1 hard-boiled egg
2 tablespoons butter	Paprika
1 tablespoon flour	Parsley
Monosodium glutamate	

I get a smoked fillet fresh or frozen weighing about a pound. The fish should be rinsed off in cold water and patted dry with a paper towel.

It is then poached over low heat in milk in a skillet or frying pan with a cover. Don't boil the milk or there will be a mess on the stove.

When the fish flakes easily with a fork, it is done. A frozen piece obviously takes a little more time.

While this is going on I make a roux in the top of a double boiler over a low flame. For two people I use two tablespoons of butter. One tablespoon of flour.

When the fish is done, I drain the poaching milk into the roux to make the usual white sauce, adding a little monosodium glutamate and white pepper.

Break the fish into pieces and fold into the sauce and add a chopped hard-boiled egg. I serve it over a toasted English muffin with a sprinkling of paprika and chopped parsley.

Codfish Cakes

(Serves 4-6)

Although codfish cakes may be bought frozen or in tins, they cannot compare with the homemade variety. To start from scratch, salt cod is necessary. Formerly it could be obtained in wooden boxes put out by Gorton's of Boston. In my youth we nibbled torn off strips, salt and all and called it Boston Candy. Today, as far as I can find out, the wooden boxes have vanished. It is now sold in cans or in one-pound plastic-wrapped packages.

1 pound salt codfish	Pepper
Boiled potatoes	Monosodium glutamate
2 eggs	Vegetable oil
Salt	

Wash the codfish in several changes of water and soak overnight in cold water in the refrigerator. Before using, wring it out dry in cheesecloth. Cut into small pieces and put through the fine blade of the meat grinder.

Have available five or six boiled potatoes without their skins.

Mash them well and combine them with the ground-up fish, 2 raw eggs, salt, pepper, and a pinch of monosodium glutamate.

This mixture freezes well. I usually make up a batch, mold it into patties, and store in a freezer container with wax paper between each one.

If planning to use them for breakfast thaw them out overnight. Roll into balls about the size of a golf ball and fry in hot vegetable oil.

I use a Chinese wok or a modified version of one that has a sort of little shelf on the side. As the codfish balls brown, which they quickly do, I draw them up onto the shelf to drain. They are crisp, non-greasy, and very good. Some people like chili sauce or ketchup with them, but I prefer them straight.

Pancakes

(Serves three, or two people and one dog)

1 cup flour	1 egg
1 teaspoon baking powder	1 tablespoon safflower or other
½ teaspoon salt	oil
Monosodium glutamate	Milk

Mix together the flour, baking powder, salt, dash of monosodium glutamate, and the egg. Then slowly add the oil and enough milk until the batter is thin but gooey. Keep stirring, but it is not necessary to smooth out all of the small lumps.

For cooking I use a soapstone griddle. One from Vermont. It does not require greasing. Have it very hot. A drop of water will dance and vanish.

Ilka has a small appetite for breakfast, so I use about 1 tablespoon of batter for each cake. Turn when well mottled with bubbles and brown on the down side. Serve with butter, maple syrup, sausages and/or bacon.

Buckwheat cakes are made the same way but using about a third of white flour to two thirds of buckwheat flour.

New England Clam Chowder

(Serves 6)

Hard-shell clams—eighteen if the size of cherrystones, 24 if little-neck size, or a few more if you wish
½ cup of raw oatmeal (if you have dug them yourself)
8 new potatoes
4 strips bacon
2 or 3 onions
1 pint milk or ½ pint fresh milk and ½ pint evaporated
1 small tin chopped clams
Salt, pepper
Dash of monosodium glutamate
Butter
Paprika

If you buy your clams the next step is not necessary. If you dig them yourself, as we frequently do, follow instructions.

Soak them for two or three hours in a gallon of salt water with a good handful of raw oatmeal added. Remove and scrub thoroughly with a hard brush.

In the meantime boil 8 new potatoes, golf-ball size. When cooked, remove skins and set aside. Brown 4 strips of bacon until crisp. Chop two or three onions, depending on size, and sauté in the bacon fat until translucent and golden. Drain off fat and set onions aside.

If you open the clams raw, keep them in their juice. If you steam them open in a little water in a covered pot, remove them from their shells and leave them in the broth.

Now for the chowder. Pour a pint of milk into the top of a double boiler. Some people prefer half fresh milk and half evaporated. Add the potatoes diced, the bacon crumbled and the clam juice or broth. Add the fried onions and cook gently in the double boiler without boiling the milk. Then add the clams. If you put them in too soon they will toughen. Also you may add a small tin of chopped clams, which gives a little additional zest. Add salt, pepper to taste and a little monosodium glutamate. Pour into a tureen or individual soup bowls, float a bit of butter on top, sprinkle with paprika, and serve. Corn bread is a fine accompaniment.

Herewith the butterfly lamb on the outdoor grill.

Butterfly Lamb
(Serves 6–8)

Leg of lamb	Salt and pepper
Olive oil	Garlic
Red wine	Rosemary

Have your butcher split and bone a leg of lamb. Marinate it overnight or for several hours in a shallow baking dish in half a cup of olive oil, enough red wine just to cover, salt, freshly ground pepper, a crushed garlic clove or two and a pinch of dried rosemary leaves or fresh ones if available.

Prepare your outdoor grill, and when the flame has died down and the coals are both gray and glowing underneath, place the meat on the grill, fat side down. It is a good idea to have a bowl of water and a baster handy so that if fat drips onto the coals you can extinguish any flame that shoots up.

After about fifteen minutes turn the meat. It is hard to give the exact time since doneness is a matter of taste, but we like it best when it is brown and crispy on the outside and still pink within. I usually allow about twenty-three minutes.

At one period in our lives, it wasn't too long, six weeks to two months, I should say, we lived high on the hog. That is perhaps not the most graceful turn of phrase available since the agent responsible for our lofty faring was Ann Willan, an attractive, well-bred English girl who had decided to become a professional cook. She had studied and worked in France and London and when she first came to this country she took a temporary live-in job. We heard of her through a friend, and she agreed to come to us for a little while.

She made great soufflés, which I myself have yet to master, but two of her dishes we adopted permanently and they are a part of our eating pattern.

One is very easy and an unexpected and refreshing entree to a summer dinner.

Fruit Entree

Melon balls	Oil
White grapes	Vinegar
Tom Thumb tomatoes	Salt and pepper

Take cantaloupe or honeydew melon. Scoop meat into balls. Mix with white grapes and Tom Thumb tomatoes. Use the smallest possible or, if they are on the large side, cut in half. Toss together with a simple French dressing made with the oil and vinegar, salt and pepper—you might add a little fresh mint or tarragon if you have any in the garden—and serve in the cantaloupe shells.

Sometimes if the shells are big, it may seem too substantial a first course. In that case serve in small bowls.

Another Ann Willan contribution we cherish is a dessert, a very special affair and one that I have got the knack of.

Ann Willan's Peach Cake with Nut Flour

(Serves 6-8)

Cake layer:

1 cup nut flour (see method)	¾ cup butter, softened
1 cup all-purpose flour	1 cup granulated sugar

Filling:

8 fresh peaches	1 pint heavy cream
½ cup water	Kirsch
1 cup granulated sugar	Confectioners' sugar
1 piece vanilla bean	

Preheat oven to 350° F. To make nut flour, brown hazelnuts on baking sheet in oven. (Almonds are also very good and easier to find, but hazelnuts are special.) Put through meat grinder or

141

blender until fine as coarse meal (you should have 1 cup ground nuts). Place in mixing bowl with flour, butter, and 1 cup sugar. Mix together to form a dough. When well blended and firm enough to form a ball, divide into 3 parts. With the heel of the hand, on a baking sheet, press out each section until it forms a circle approximately 7¾ inches. Bake for about 15 minutes or until brown. Dough will spread a little. Cut into perfect circles with the lid of a Revere saucepan or the equivalent. Cool on baking sheet, but while still warm, slip a spatula between the nut crust and baking sheet to loosen.

Meanwhile, combine the water, 1 cup sugar, and vanilla bean in a saucepan. Add peaches, stew gently until soft and skin can be pinched off. Remove from syrup, quarter, and set aside.

To assemble, whip the cream; add kirsch and confectioners' sugar to taste. Place 1 nut crust on a *flat-bottomed* serving plate. Divide whipped cream into 4 parts. Top the crust with ¼ of the whipped cream, 16 peach quarters, another ¼ of whipped cream, and another nut crust. Repeat these layers and sprinkle top crust with confectioners' sugar. This should be made only a few hours before eating.

As I said I have learned to concoct the above Wow, and if driven to it I can occasionally manage another sumptuous dessert: cheese cake. There are many recipes for this but the following is particularly seductive and whenever we buy Zweiback for the crust in our local market chops are licked and hands extended like Oliver Twist begging for just *one* helping and they'll forgo the more.

Cheese Cake

(Serves 10–12)

Crust:

1½ cups Zweiback crumbs	1 teaspoon cinnamon
¼ cup granulated sugar	½ cup melted butter

Filling:

2 pounds cream cheese, softened   Pinch of salt
1¼ cups granulated sugar   1 pint sour cream
4 eggs, well beaten   1 teaspoon vanilla
1 tablespoon lemon juice

Preheat oven to 375° F. To make crust, combine all crust ingredients; mix well. Press about ¾ of the mixture onto the bottom and sides of a 10-inch spring-form pan. To make filling: cream the cheese. Add 1 cup of the sugar to the eggs, beating until thick and lemon-colored. Add to the cheese with the lemon juice and salt. Beat well with rotary beater; pour into the prepared pan. Bake for 20 minutes. Meanwhile, combine the sour cream, remaining ¼ cup sugar, and vanilla. Spread over the partially baked cake and sprinkle with the remaining crumbs. Increase oven temperature to 475° F. and bake 10 minutes. Remove from oven and cool. Then refrigerate several hours. Remove from refrigerator 1 hour before serving.

You never know where luck, like lightning, may strike. When Norton and I were in Korolevu, a seaside resort in the Fiji Islands* we encountered a delightful American couple, Dean and Donald Stewart.

At that time they lived in Independence, Kansas—they have since moved to Springfield, Missouri—but they were as sophisticated a pair of world travelers as you would ever meet were you to circle the globe continuously for a year on end.

Dean is a tiny creature with a heart full of affection and humor and a skull full of brains. There is nothing the matter with her palate either.

The four of us struck up a fine friendship, and Dean and I still write to each other. She is a better correspondent than I, but I appreciate her bounty. When I told her I was writing this book she sent me the two following recipes. Her memo on the first one reads: "Every family on the coast line from Baltimore to Brownsville has its own gumbo recipe. This is our family's."

* *Second Spring and Two Potatoes*

Sea Food Gumbo

(Serves 6–8)

2 ounces salt pork, cubed
1 large onion, finely chopped
2 tablespoons salad oil
2 tablespoons flour
1 can (1 pound) peeled
 tomatoes
1 can (15½ ounces) okra
2 cups water
1 can (8 ounces) mushrooms,
 drained

1 can (4 ounces) cove oysters
 or ½ pint fresh oysters
1 can (8 ounces) lump crabmeat or ½ pound fresh or
 frozen cooked crabmeat
2 cans (4½ ounces) shrimp or
 ½ pound raw shrimp, shelled
2 tablespoons gumbo filé

In a 4-quart kettle, sauté cubed salt pork and onion in the oil until onion is tender; remove pork. Add flour, stirring until all fat is absorbed. Add tomatoes, okra, and water; simmer, covered, 3 to 4 hours. About 10 minutes before serving, add mushrooms, sea food (with its liquid), and gumbo filé. Most stores that have good spice racks sell this. Blend everything together well, cover, and simmer till heated through. Spoon over cooked rice.

Dean Stewart's other dish is

Apricot Torte

(Serves 6–8)

Short Pastry (Many cook books have good recipes for this)

Apricot Topping:
2 cups (11 ounces) dried
 apricots
2 cups water

1 cup granulated sugar
¼ teaspoon nutmeg
¼ teaspoon cinnamon

Sauce:
Liquid from cooked apricots
 (about ⅓ cup)

1 teaspoon sugar (or more,
 according to taste)
2 tablespoons lemon juice

Preheat oven to 350° F. Place pastry in bottom and ½ inch up the sides of an 8-inch square pan. To make the topping, combine apricots and water; cook, covered, 10 to 15 minutes or until mushy. Drain juice and reserve for sauce. To the cooked apricots add the 1 cup sugar, nutmeg, and cinnamon; mix well. Spread over crust in pan. Bake 25 to 30 minutes.

Meanwhile, combine the cooked apricot liquid with the teaspoon of sugar and lemon juice in small saucepan. Cook over low heat till sugar dissolves. Pour over dessert and serve hot. Do not reheat sauce as it will crystallize.

Mrs. Stewart adds, "That's all there is, but don't knock it till you've tried it."

In many books that deal with food or the well-equipped household there are suggestions for provisions to be kept on hand. It is an intelligent system in which many people concur.

With refrigerated storage we are no longer confined to the obvious staples—salt, pepper, flour, sugar, tea, coffee, cocoa, etc., and an enormous variety of canned goods—we can maintain a quite dazzling selection of frozen delicacies as well.

I understand this, and every once in a while I scuttle about, laying in supplies, frozen and otherwise. I seem to have an addiction for rice, not shared, I may say, by my dear husband. But given enough rice I apparently feel I can face Armaggedon. It's a rare day in our house that we lack the great staple of Asia.

Even at that, however, we occasionally fall upon sparse times when there seems to be very little with which to concoct an extemporaneous meal. For the humans, that is. The animals have it made!

For our too plump dachshund, Belinda, there are diet foods and Alpo and a spectacular variety of biscuits. Spice, the cat, does even better. Spice is spoiled, and while there is always a supply of tinned cat food for a rainy day, our deep freeze seems to have been acquired largely as a storage space for drumsticks, chicken gizzards and hearts, chunks of beef liver, and fish.

Indeed one day, having observed our own pickings, distinctly on the slim side, Norton suddenly brightened. "We can always invade Spice's locker," he said, "and we'll do pretty well."

Still, we're not beholden to him. We have some meals which, while Escoffier might not envy them, keep body and soul together. Leftovers. Steak sandwiches and Brussels sprout salad. Roast beef hash. A fried-egg sandwich and leftover plum pudding. Sliced ham and remnants of the peaches from Ann Willans' great hazelnut flour and peach dessert. You don't *plan* such meals, they just happen.

When I was a child I once had a supper consisting entirely of nine ears of fresh garden corn. Greatest food I ever ate.

It doesn't have to be snazzy. It just has to taste good.

The goodies now coming up are distinctly tasty and snazzy to boot.

My friend Ruth Anderson has got to be doing something right. She knows two men, Mr. Kenny Bates and Mr. Dick McKay, who are frequent weekend visitors in her house and they are both dedicated cooks. How many women can say as much? A few of their recipes follow. The first one sounds mad, I grant you but just you try it.

Creamed Spinach Folie

(Serves 4)

2 pounds fresh spinach	Nutmeg
½ cup boiling water	2–4 tablespoons chives
2 tablespoons butter	¼ cup heavy cream, whipped
2 tablespoons flour	Grated Parmesan cheese
1 cup milk	Butter
Salt and pepper to taste	

Discard any yellow or wilted leaves. Remove all stems. Wash thoroughly to remove sand; drain well. Cook in boiling water, about 5 minutes, or until tender. Drain thoroughly and press to get all water out; chop.

Meanwhile, make rich sauce by melting butter in saucepan over low heat. Add flour gradually, blending without browning.

Stir in milk, stirring constantly. Continue to cook and stir until smooth. Simmer for another 5 minutes and continue to stir over low heat to avoid an uncooked flour flavor. Season to taste with the salt, pepper, and nutmeg, and add chives. Blend in the chopped spinach. Spoon into a shallow 1-quart casserole. Spread with lightly salted whipped cream; sprinkle with grated Parmesan and dot with butter. Place under broiler until puffy and sizzling brown.

This recipe comes from the Auberge de Nove in Provence "which," says Kenny Bates, "is, for my money, a great restaurant. Especially if you are there at the right time and can eat outside under the peach trees all in flower."

What follows is also from the same auberge. The management would not divulge the secret of its composition but the Messrs. Bates and McKay are not men to be defeated by managerial secrecy. They futzed around on their own for a while and herewith the irresistible result. It's a dessert, by the way, as you will quickly see.

Bombe Praline

(Serves 8)

½ cup slivered almonds	Jamaica rum or brandy
2½ cups granulated sugar	½ teaspoon cream of tartar
1 cup water	8 egg yolks
¾ cup raisins	1 cup heavy cream, whipped
Boiling water	

Toast almonds on baking sheet in oven until brown. Combine ½ cup sugar and ¼ cup water in heavy saucepan; boil until caramelized. Stir in toasted almonds. Pour onto a well-buttered baking sheet; cool. When hard, pulverize in a blender.

Soak the raisins in boiling water until plump; drain. Place in bowl and cover with rum or brandy; set aside.

In large, heavy-bottomed saucepan, combine the remaining 2 cups sugar, ¾ cup water, and cream of tartar. Bring to a boil and cook rapidly until syrup spins a light thread—232° F. on a candy thermometer. In top of a double boiler, beat yolks until pale yellow. Continue beating and very slowly add 1 cup of the syrup. This requires three hands or a kitchen aid appliance. Cook in the double boiler, stirring constantly, until smooth. If, despite your efforts, it remains a bit lumpy, strain through a sieve then beat over ice until cool. The ice is important, as it stops the cooking. Fold in the whipped cream. Fold in the praline and most of the raisins, drained, leaving some for garnish. (Reserve rum or brandy for chocolate sauce.)

Pour the mixture into a lightly oiled 1-quart bombe-shaped mold. Cover the open top of the mold with foil. Freeze at least 24 hours.

To serve, dip bombe quickly in hot water and unmold onto a flat dish. Surround with remaining raisins and pour over it a warm chocolate sauce. Eat it, sigh, lie down, and die.

Chocolate Sauce

(Makes about 1 cup)

2 squares bitter chocolate
1½ cups granulated sugar
¾ cup light cream
⅓ cup hot water
1 tablespoon butter

Pinch of salt
1 teaspoon vanilla
Rum or brandy (from bombe
praline recipe)

In the top of a double boiler, melt chocolate. Add the sugar, cream, water, butter, and salt. Cook for 10 minutes. Add the vanilla and some of the rum or brandy, depending on whichever you used to soak the raisins in the previous recipe. Just don't let it thin out the sauce too much. Stir and serve hot.

Less of a razzmatazz but equally delicious in its innocent way is this.

Almond Ring

(Serves 6–8)

½ cup Zweiback crumbs 1⅔ cups ground almonds
1¼ cups granulated sugar ½ teaspoon almond extract
4 egg whites

Preheat oven to 325° F. Combine the Zweiback crumbs, and ¼ cup of the sugar. Sprinkle half the mixture over the inside of a heavily buttered 1-quart ring mold. Set aside. Reserve remaining crumb mixture for topping.

Beat the egg whites until stiff; add the remaining 1 cup sugar, a little at a time, beating well after each addition. Continue beating until stiff peaks form. Gradually fold in the ground almonds and the almond extract. Spoon into the prepared ring mold and spread Zweiback crumbs on top.

Place in oven and bake 30 to 35 minutes. Turn oven off, and cool cake in oven with the door ajar. If it sticks, and it will, very carefully loosen edges with knife and invert onto a serving dish. Fill the center with your favorite sherbet. Raspberry or lemon with fresh or thawed frozen raspberries over it is particularly nice.

There are types for whom apples conjure up Adam and Eve. Others, when they see or think about them, remember their childhood. I am one of these. Grandma used to give me scraped apple. Scraped apple scarcely requires a recipe. You cut an apple in half and scrape it out with a spoon. Simple. Yet nevertheless it requires a certain technique. You must scrape. Not scoop. I don't know why it tasted so good. Maybe because someone else was doing the work and because I loved Grandma. My grandmother was a Quaker and Mother and I always used "thee" and "thy" when speaking with her. However, she was a peppery little party and the benignity usually associated with the Quaker sect was foreign to her nature. She believed in carrying the battle to the enemy and it was uncanny the frequency with which her daughter and granddaughter seemed to fit the category. As I grew so did our differences, but in my childhood my relationship with Grandma was sunny and serene.

This following somewhat more sophisticated but still simple trick with apples I owe to Dick McKay.

Stewed Apples

(Serves 4)

4 apples	1½ cups firmly packed dark
Lemon juice	brown sugar
	1½ sticks butter

Peel and core your apples, the number depending on the number of partakers. Sour apples are fine and so are McIntosh. Depending on size, cut into six or eight sections—you don't want them too small—and douse liberally with lemon juice. This keeps them from discoloring and improves the flavor.

In a large frying pan melt together 1½ cups of brown sugar and 1½ sticks of butter. Blend and stir until syrupy. Place apples in the sauce and simmer very slowly turning them at least once. Don't let them disintegrate. They should remain firm but be cooked inside their sugar casing.

While still warm place in individual dessert bowls and pass with heavy cream.

I am a great fan of fruit desserts, fresh or cooked but as A. A. Milne's king observed to his queen: "I do like a little bit of butter to my bread," so do I like a little bit of cookie to my fruit. These are good.

Oatmeal Cookies

(Makes 9 dozen)

½ cup shortening
½ cup butter
1 cup firmly packed light brown sugar
1 cup granulated sugar
1 egg

1 teaspoon vanilla
¼ cup molasses
2 cups quick-cooking Quaker oats
½ cup flour
⅛ teaspoon baking soda

Preheat oven to 325° F. Cream shortening and butter; add sugars, then egg, vanilla, and molasses, blending until smooth. Combine oatmeal, flour, and baking soda; add to creamed mixture. Blend well. Drop by level teaspoonfuls, 2½ to 3 inches apart, onto an ungreased baking sheet. (Cookies spread thin during baking.) Bake 8 to 10 minutes.

Because of the molasses they will be bubbling a bit when you remove them from the oven. Let stand just long enough to calm down (about 1 to 2 minutes), then attack quickly yet deftly and loosen them with a spatula. Place on rack to cool. The whole batter may be blended in an electric mixer.

That Mr. McKay has a sweet tooth and in this instance we are the winners. As he says, "Very southern, this one and pretty damned good."

Blackberry Jam Cake

(Makes 2 9-inch layers)

1 scant cup butter, softened
1 scant cup granulated sugar
3 eggs
1 teaspoon baking soda
1½ cups buttermilk
2 cups sifted flour

1 teaspoon baking powder
1 teaspoon cinnamon
1 teaspoon ground cloves
1 teaspoon allspice
1 cup (12-ounce jar) blackberry jam

Preheat oven to 350° F. Grease and lightly flour 2 9-inch round cake pans. Blend butter and sugar until light and creamy. Add eggs one at a time, beating after each addition. Dissolve soda in buttermilk; combine remaining ingredients except blackberry jam. Stir dry ingredients and buttermilk alternately into the creamed mixture. When well blended, stir in *by hand slowly and thoroughly* the blackberry jam. Mixture will have a very curdled appearance, but don't be frightened. Pour half the batter into each pan; bake 30 to 35 minutes or until a cake tester comes out moist. Not dry.

Remove from pans and cool on a rack. "In the meantime make your favorite caramel icing," says Mr. McKay. Up until now I haven't had a favorite, but I do like the lady say in *The Joy of Cooking* and I suggest you do the same.

Miniature Tarts for Fresh Fruit

When we had our cook, Kathleen, the one who was a demon for working alone, she made a dessert that I had never seen in that form before and only in my own house since. It was fruit tarts but tiny little ones baked in bite-sized individual tartpans.

When cooked they were filled with an assortment of fruit. One strawberry in one, a couple of grapes in another, three or four blueberries, a slice of banana, two or three raspberries, a cherry . . . the idea is to have as much variety as possible. The fruit was raw but covered with an apricot glaze made by straining apricot preserves through a sieve, mixing them with a little fine sugar and boiling the mixture quickly until it coats the spoon. It should be applied to the fruit while still warm.

Served on a large flat plate, the tarts are a pretty sight and people take a childlike pleasure in helping themselves to five or six of their favorites.

But enough of sweetmeats for a while. On to sterner stuff. The following is a lulu. It comes from Tennessee and it's called

Cawn Puddin

(Serves 6–8)

1 No. 2 can cream-style corn	1 tablespoon sugar
5 eggs, well beaten	1 teaspoon salt
3 cups milk	1 tablespoon cornstarch
3 tablespoons melted butter	

Preheat oven to 350° F. Butter a 1½-quart soufflé dish. Combine all ingredients except cornstarch; blend well. Blend cornstarch with a small amount of water to make a smooth paste; blend into corn mixture. Pour into the prepared soufflé dish; bake 1 hour. Supposedly this will serve 6 to 8, but Kenny Bates says, "I've seen four people polish off the whole thing.

The same Mr. Bates contrived the following for a buffet luncheon on a hot summer's day.

Tomato Aspic

(Serves 10–12)

2 packages unflavored gelatin	4 cans (6 ounces each) Snap-E-Tom (this is a highly
¼ cup lemon juice	seasoned tomato juice
1 package (3 ounces) lemon Jell-O	available in most grocery
1 can (46 ounces) V-8 juice	stores)

In a large bowl, soften the unflavored gelatin in the lemon juice. Add the lemon Jell-O. Bring 2 cups of the V-8 to a boil; pour over mixture in bowl, stirring until gelatins are dissolved. Add remaining ingredients. Pour into a lightly oiled 9-cup mold. Cool and chill for several hours; overnight is better. (Use a large, fairly flat mold; if a tall mold is used, add 1 more envelope of unflavored gelatin.)

The contriver then adds: "If you don't want so much, half the recipe will do. Cut down some on the V-8 and divide the rest by two. Except for the Snap-E-Tom. The more the snappier. It's a very elastic thing. If you hit one of those awful days when nothing will jell, heat up the whole thing again and add another package of gelatin. It won't affect the flavor and the damned thing will hold together."

For other aspics I am indebted to a lady who for many years was known as The Face. The beautiful Miss Anita Colby who is now the beautiful Mrs. Palen Flagler. In her premarital days, although a sophisticated and experienced consumer, I believe she was not all that devoted to the range, but since her marriage she has become a demon chef. Her invitations to dine or spend a weekend are eagerly accepted, yet the invited groan, knowing full well they will have gained five to ten pounds from ingesting her hospitality. The following is not all that fattening but it is all that delicious and it is easy to make.

I must admit that in trying it out I deviated a little bit to come up with what is here, but the idea was Mrs. Flagler's. She was the source!

Clam Aspic

(Serves 4)

I made this for a small circular mold that held just under a pint and a half.

1 dozen cherrystone clams and their juice (about ¾ cup liquid)	Salt and pepper to taste
	1 envelope plus ¾ teaspoon unflavored gelatin
½ cup chicken broth	Sour cream
¼ cup white wine	Caviar or cucumbers
2 tablespoons lemon juice	

The difference between caviar and cucumbers is considerable but will be explained. I have tried doing this with canned minced clams but they were not satisfactory. Too tough.

Remove the fresh clams from their shells yourself or have the fish man do it. Either way, *keep the juice.* Drain it from the clams and mix with the chicken broth, white wine, lemon juice and salt and pepper. Sprinkle the gelatin over ½ cup of this liquid to soften. Bring rest of liquid to a boil. Add softened gelatin, stirring until gelatin dissolves. Finely mince the clams (about ¾ cup), spread them on bottom of a 3-cup mold which you have rinsed out in cold water. Add the hot liquid. Cool, then refrigerate until jelled.

When ready to serve, turn out onto flat plate and fill with sour cream mixed with caviar. The caviar elegance is Mrs. Flagler's. Most budgets won't stretch that far. Happily the more plebeian limp, paper-thin slices of cucumber mixed with sour cream is mine, and it's good, if I do say so.

You could also use crab meat instead of clams and lime juice rather than lemon and increase chicken broth to 1¼ cups.

I imagine most people know how to limp cucumbers but it took me a long time to learn. In case any newcomers are as ignorant as I was, here's what you do. Peel and slice your cucumber as thin as possible to begin with. A cole slaw slicer—that wooden board with an adjustable blade in the center—is ideal, but watch it! You can get a nasty cut. Spread your slices out on a fair-sized plate and salt them heavily to draw out the water. Cover with Saran Wrap and put in the refrigerator for an hour or so. Longer doesn't hurt. When ready to use, dump them into a sieve and rinse thoroughly under cold running water. Pat dry and go ahead with any plan you have in mind.

Another aspic that she generously passed on to me Anita Flagler learned at the Jockey Club in Madrid. They eat well at the Jockey Club, as I know from experience,* and this recipe is worth while.

* *The Carthaginian Rose*

Chicken Livers in Aspic

(Makes about 3 cups)

1 pound chicken livers
¼ cup minced onion
1 tablespoon butter
1 tablespoon brandy
1 teaspoon of beef extract or
Bovril

1 envelope unflavored gelatin
1 can (10½ ounces) condensed
consommé

Remove membrane from chicken livers; dry thoroughly with paper toweling. Sauté the livers and onion in butter till livers are brown on outside but still pink inside. Remove from heat; mash or put through fine blade of food chopper (about 2 cups mixture, loosely packed). Add brandy and beef flavoring. Soften the gelatin in ¼ cup of the consommé. Heat remaining consommé to boiling; add softened gelatin, stirring till gelatin dissolves. Blend into chicken-liver mixture. Pour into a lightly oiled 3 cup mold. For this you are probably better off with a solid block than with a ring mold. Refrigerate overnight or several hours until set. Serve at cocktail time with crackers or toast fingers.

Chicken in Aspic

(Serves 6 to 8)

1 4- to 5-pound stewing chicken,
cut into pieces
4–5 ribs celery, with leaves
1 bay leaf
Few sprigs parsley
½ cup chopped onion
8 peppercorns

2 envelopes unflavored gelatin
¼ cup cold water
Tarragon
Sliced stuffed and/or pitted
black olives
2 cans pâté de foie gras

Place chicken in large kettle; cover with cold water. Bring to a boil; reduce heat and simmer, covered, for 2½ hours. Add celery, bay leaf, parsley, onion, and peppercorns and simmer about ½ hour more or until chicken is tender. Remove chicken from broth;

cool; and remove meat from bones. Boil broth till it reduces to 3 cups. Clarify by adding 1 slightly beaten egg white. Bring to the boil again; remove from heat. When cool, skim fat from surface. Strain broth, return to heat and bring to a boil. Soften the gelatin in cold water; add to boiling broth, remove from heat and stir until gelatin dissolves. Rinse a 6-cup mold with cold water. Pour in gelatin to ¼-inch thickness; chill until mixture begins to jell. Place on gelatin a pattern of the tarragon and sliced olives. Pour on a thin coating of gelatin; chill till almost set. Top with pieces of chicken; spread with pâté; cover with remaining gelatin and chill until set.

When ready to serve run a knife around the edge, dip for an instant in hot water and unmold on a bed of lettuce.

With this Anita Flagler serves vegetable salad, sometimes going to the trouble of making little individual molds of jellied vegetables and setting them around the central *pièce de résistance*. Serve with mayonnaise if so minded.

Ruth Anderson is a good friend of Anita Colby Flager's. Indeed it was she who told me about the aspics she had eaten in Anita's house, and is herself no mean hand at the pots.

She frequently serves aspics on summer weekends. It was on one of those occasions that the well-fed guests fell to musing on life's frustrations.

It was a Sunday, and that morning two or three of them, accompanied by the hostess, had gone to the village church. The church was picturesque—the chief reason for the attendance—and prettily set at the edge of a small lake, but a sign they had noticed disturbed the temporarily devout. It sternly admonished, NO FISHING. NO SWIMMING.

Mrs. Anderson and her friends felt that was not a very Christian attitude and if there was going to be so much interdiction they might as well cinch the deal. They accordingly spent an industrious hour carefully blocking and printing a prohibition of their own which, subsequently and surreptitiously, they nailed to the post below the other two. Theirs read: NO WALKING ON WATER.

The following contribution is from Ruth Anderson and is the reverse of the aspic coin, best appreciated in cold weather. Mighty savory it is.

It can of course be curtailed to serve a smaller number, but it is great food for a generous-sized group, say twenty to twenty-four people, and it has two vast virtues: deliciousness and simplicity of preparation. Ruth Anderson serves it on New Year's Eve along with green noodles. Its drawback is that you must use an expensive cut of meat. Top sirloin is best. It is better made the day before and reheated.

Beef and Onions
(Serves 20–24)

10 pounds top sirloin	Onions
Butter	Paprika
Vegetable oil	Salt and pepper

Order from the butcher ten pounds of top sirloin cut into beef-stew-sized pieces. Sear the pieces, a batch at a time, in butter and vegetable oil, but do not cook through. Remove and drain them.

Chop coarsely enough onions to fill a big iron pot about a quarter of the way up. Put the meat on top of the onions, sprinkle very generously with the best Hungarian paprika, salt, and freshly ground black pepper. Cover tightly and set over a high flame until the onions begin to bubble a bit—then reduce to a simmer. Depending on the amount in the pot it will take 2 to 4 hours to cook. Remove when the meat is still pink and juicy on the inside. The onions will have miraculously disappeared leaving only juice.

Wauhillau Lahay is ranking member of the Washington press corps. She is a confidante of First Ladies, a good friend of Ruth Anderson's, and one who enjoys luscious eats. Herewith a few of her favorites, which she kindly jotted down for me, giving up several hours of her brief summer holiday to do so. Let us all join in expressions of gratitude. This is her suggestion for a cold-weather buffet. She calls this a quick cassoulet. It still takes time.

Cassoulet

(Serves 16–18)

6 cans (15 ounces) navy beans *or*	2 pork tenderloins (6–8 inches long)
6 cans (12½ ounces) flageolets	Lemon-pepper seasoning
1 onion, cut in half	2 whole, boned chicken breasts
2 stalks celery	½-pound piece Canadian bacon
Bouquet garni (thyme, bay leaf, and parsley)	½ pound hot Italian sausage
	½ pound link sausage
1 can (8 ounces) tomato sauce	Buttered bread cubes
¼ pound salt pork	

Mrs. Lahay says you can use the navy beans or flageolets, but she herself prefers the navy.

Place the beans in a heavy pot, add onion, celery, and bouquet garni in a cheesecloth package so it may be removed later on. Simmer for 1 hour. Stir in the tomato sauce.

Meanwhile, soak the salt pork in ice water for an hour. Rub the pork tenderloins with lemon-pepper seasoning and bake at 350° F. for 1 hour. Place chicken breasts and Canadian bacon in water to cover and boil till chicken is tender. When cooked, thinly slice the pork tenderloin, bacon, and chicken breast. Remove casing from hot sausage and cook till done; pour off all fat. Dry salt pork, dice, and fry out. Do not cook link sausage, slice thinly. Layer ingredients in two 3-quart casseroles, alternating beans, meat, beans, meat. Top with the diced salt pork and chunky buttered bread cubes. This may all be done and assembled ahead of time.

When getting ready to serve, bake in a 350° F. oven for 1 hour. "Or more," says Mrs. Lahay, "depending on the drinking capacity of your guests. It's a big, hearty dish, nice and fattening."

With this she serves cole slaw made with very young cabbage, tossed with a bacon grease, cream, and vinegar dressing. Hot Mexican corn bread goes well with it. To any good corn-bread mix add grated Cheddar cheese and grated onion. Make muffins or sticks.

Fruit and cheese for dessert. With this particular meal beer is better than wine.

Another Lahay contribution. This one discovered in Cuba. When Norton and I tried it out one evening we did it just for ourselves, so the amounts were small. One would of course increase them for more people.

Almejas Verdes (Green Clams)

(Serves 2)

¼ cup butter
2–3 cloves garlic, finely crushed
1–2 tablespoons chopped fresh
    parsley

1 can condensed green-pea soup
2 dozen cherrystone clams (with
    clam liquor)

You can steam the clams open, but this tends to toughen them. The better way is to remove them from the shells while raw. As this is something of a chore, you might have your kindly neighborhood fish man do it for you. Whoever does it, reserve the juice, which is vital. You will want at least 1 dozen claims per person.

Into a heavy pot, place the butter, garlic, parsley, clam broth (about 1¼ cups), and the pea soup. Stir together; bring to a boil. Reduce heat and let simmer just a bit. Add the clams, and as soon as they are heated through—you don't want to overcook them— pour into a tureen or individual soup bowls.

Served with crusty French bread and perhaps a salad followed by fruit, this is a meal in itself. The drink companion: a dry white wine.

Summer Squash à Lahay

(Serves 4)

3 medium yellow squash	1–2 tablespoons milk
2 medium onions, finely chopped	1 tablespoon chopped fresh dill
1 tablespoon butter	Paprika
1 pint sour cream	Salt and pepper to taste
1 tablespoon flour	

Peel and dice the squash and cook in salted water until they are just al dente, not mushy. Drain.

Sauté onions in butter until golden. Pour sour cream into the top of a double boiler or a heavy pan such as a Creuset. Keep stirring, and when it bubbles add the flour and milk which have been mixed to form a smooth paste. Cook about 5 minutes or so until the raw flour taste has disappeared.

Add the fresh dill, a generous dusting of paprika, salt and pepper. Get *good* paprika. It makes all the difference.

Combine the squash and cream mixture. Heat through and serve. This can be made a day ahead and reheated. Mrs. Lahay's comment on the above is accurate. "I must say it looks like pineapple in whipped cream, but it tastes divine."

Anyone in, or interested in, the theatre will know the name Armina Marshall Langner. She is the widow of the late Lawrence Langner, a director of the Theatre Guild in that organization's heyday, when Guild productions were considered the cream of the American stage.

Armina was an actress herself, and together she and Lawrence wrote several plays. Not only did they provide actors with work, Miss Marshall provided them with food, comfort, advice, and encouragement.

Everyone wanted to be invited to the Langners' Sunday night buffet parties. They were on Sundays because, hopefully, most of the celebrated names would be working in plays on Broadway on week nights. Actors, playwrights, even an occasional critic, hobnobbed together. This they thought would help their careers. They *knew* without doubt that the food would help their well-being.

Lawrence died in 1962, but Armina still maintains to some degree the delicious buffet tradition.

The following dish stars as a first course, or Armina often serves it with cocktails. It is also a star in the Anne Roe Robbins Cooking School.

Cold Shrimp with Sauce

Shell and devein 2 pounds raw shrimp. Bring enough water to a boil to cover the shrimp, with a slice of lemon and a little salt. Put in the shrimp and cook for 3 minutes after the water has come to a boil again. Drain and while still hot put into French dressing to marinate, using 3 parts of olive oil to 1 part lemon juice, and a little dry mustard and salt. Let cool. If the shrimp are to wait for any time before being served, place them covered in the refrigerator. However they taste better when they are not ice cold, so I suggest leaving them half an hour at room temperature before serving. Drain well and serve with one or both of the following sauces. They should be made several hours ahead of time or the day before and chilled in the refrigerator.

Shrimp Sauce 1

½ cup mayonnaise, preferably homemade
½ cup sour cream
1 tablespoon lemon juice
1 teaspoon grated onion
1 teaspoon dry mustard
2 tablespoons chopped parsley or dill *or*
1 tablespoon each

Blend all of the ingredients together, taste for seasoning, and chill covered for several hours or until ready to serve.

Shrimp Sauce 2

½ cup mayonnaise, preferably
    homemade
½ cup Creole mustard
1 tablespoon lemon juice

1 tablespoon grated onion
1 clove garlic, crushed
1 tablespoon finely chopped
    celery

The Creole mustard is what makes this sauce unusual. Blend all of the ingredients together, taste for seasoning, and chill covered in the refrigerator for several hours or as long as you like.

We have friends in the country, John and Mary Sulzer, who are friends indeed. Not only do they ask us to dine on everyday occasions, they take care of us at Thanksgiving and on New Year's Eve. Without a large family, holidays can sometimes be on the gloomy side but never in the welcoming atmosphere chez Sulzer. John is Swiss and the following is a favorite of his. And Mary's. And ours.

Délices d'Emmenthal

(Serves 6–8)

This recipe makes 24 croquettes and will serve 8. Allow 3 croquettes per person if used as a first course at dinner or 4 per person if used as a luncheon dish. It must be made the day before it is to be eaten.

¼ pound imported Swiss cheese
¼ pound sharp Cheddar cheese
2 cups milk
Pinch of salt and pepper

Pinch of nutmeg
1 cup sifted flour
1 egg
Oil for frying

Coarsely grate and combine the Swiss and Cheddar cheese. In a saucepan, heat milk with salt, pepper, and nutmeg. Add cheese, stirring constantly until cheese melts and mixture is smooth. Add flour gradually, while beating with a wire whisk. Beat in the egg to make a heavy dough or batter. Spoon the batter into a well-buttered 9-inch square pan. Cover and refrigerate for at least 10 hours.

Early the next day, cut dough into strips about 1 inch wide, and cut each strip into three pieces. Roll dough in floured hands to shape croquettes. Dredge in flour, beaten egg, and bread crumbs. Refrigerate until extremely cold, otherwise it will disintegrate in the hot fat in which it is cooked. Heat fat to 350° F.; add croquettes and fry a few minutes or until golden brown.

They can be frozen before frying. In that event thaw in refrigerator several hours before frying. Otherwise they are crisp on outside, but still frozen in center. Serve with tomato sauce that follows.

Tomato Sauce

(Makes about 2 cups)

Heat ½ cup of olive oil with one clove of garlic peeled and split, 1 onion finely grated, pinches of sage, rosemary, and basil. Fresh is marvelous if you have an herb bed. Otherwise dry. When everything is soft add one 8-ounce can of tomato puree and 1 teaspoon of flour. Mix well and add 1½ cups of stock or beef bouillon. Simmer covered for an hour.

Beef Roulades

(Serves 4–6)

Stuffing:

½ cup finely chopped onion	1 egg yolk
1 tablespoon butter	Salt, pepper, and nutmeg
½ cup very dry bread crumbs	to taste

Beef Rolls:

12 thin slices beef (about ¼ inch thick and 3 inches square)	2 tablespoons butter
	2 tablespoons flour
6 slices bacon	2–3 cups beef broth

In large skillet, sauté onion in the 1 tablespoon butter until tender. Remove from heat; toss with bread crumbs. Add egg yolk and seasonings; blend well and set aside.

Lay out meat; top each piece with ½ slice of partially cooked bacon and a scant tablespoon of stuffing. Roll and tie. In same skillet that you cooked stuffing, melt the 2 tablespoons butter. Add meat rolls and brown well. Remove from pan; blend in flour, then beef broth to make a gravy. Return meat to pan; cover and simmer over low heat 45 to 60 minutes, or until meat is tender. You may also make this dish using veal instead of beef. Veal requires only about 40 minutes.

Serve with buttered noodles and green salad.

The beef, or veal birds, noodles, and green salad might be followed by this airy fluff of a dessert also courtesy of Mary Sulzer.

Lemon Mousse

(Serves 6)

6 eggs, separated   ½ to ¾ cup granulated sugar
Grated rind and juice of
  2 lemons

In top of double boiler, combine egg yolks, lemon rind, juice, and sugar. Cook, stirring constantly until thick. Beat egg whites until stiff. Fold into cooked mixture. Spoon into serving bowl or individual sherbets. Cool in refrigerator.

As we all know coq au vin once seemed glamorous and very haute cuisine. Today coq au vin, especially in the quasi-French bistros of New York has been pretty well run into the ground. Yet the fact remains that it can be a delicious and wonderfully serviceable dish. Like so many other of life's endeavors, it is one's own approach and technique that count. It may be tedious or piquant. What I always say is you get *out* of things what you put *into* them. Technique without love is sterile. Apply interest and affection to the following and you will have a memorable coq au vin.

Coq au Vin

(Serves 6–8)

2 4- to 5-pound fryers, cut into pieces
½ cup (¼ pound) butter
1 pound fresh mushrooms, halved
12 small white onions, peeled
4 small carrots, scraped and cut into pieces
1 celery heart, leaves and all, cut very small

1 tablespoon chopped parsley
1 clove garlic, minced
1 bay leaf
Pinch of thyme
1 small glass brandy
3 cups California burgundy
3 tablespoons flour
Salt and freshly ground black pepper, to taste

In large skillet brown chicken in ¼ cup of the butter till golden brown. Remove chicken to a 3-quart casserole; place in oven to keep warm. Add vegetables, garlic, bay leaf, and thyme to skillet; toss until vegetables are lightly browned. Add to casserole with chicken. Pour brandy into skillet; warm it, light, and pour over chicken. Quickly pour over chicken 1½ cups of the wine which should be slightly warmed from being set on back of the stove. In skillet melt remaining ¼ cup butter; work in flour, salt, and pepper and remaining 1½ cups wine.

To be assured of a smooth sauce, pour as much wine out of the casserole as possible, draining it into the skillet. Mix well with pan juices, then pour back into the casserole. Cover casserole and bake in 300° F. oven for 1½ hours or until chicken is tender.

Allow to cool and put in refrigerator overnight. Take out next day. Remove excess butter from top and allow 1½ hours for reheating. It is best when meat is falling from the bones. Serve with rice or small boiled potatoes.

Since I myself have a passion for rice in any form I am always happy to see it appear on the table, but there are those on whom it palls, Dr. Brown being among their number. A nice change for such benighted souls, or anybody else for that matter, is barley pilaff.

Barley Pilaff

(Makes 2 cups)

1 medium onion, finely minced	½ cup pearl barley
2 tablespoons finely minced	1 cup boiling chicken broth
celery	½ cup seedless raisins
¼ cup butter	Parsley, finely chopped

Preheat oven to 350° F. In a flameproof casserole (if you don't have one, do this step in skillet and then combine with barley and chicken broth in a 1-quart casserole), sauté onion and celery in butter until vegetables are soft and translucent. Add the barley and boiling chicken broth; stir together. Bake about ½ hour, or until broth is absorbed and the barley puffed and soft. Remove from oven. Add the raisins, toss together. To serve, sprinkle with finely chopped parsley.

The next casserole has been in my files a long time and is a cross between a chowder and a stew. The flavor is subtle and delicious.

Fish Stew

(Serves 6)

2 tablespoons butter	1½ 8-ounce cans minced clams
2 shallots, minced, *or* 1 small	1¾ cups heavy cream
onion, minced	Salt and freshly ground
1½ pounds of sole, scrod, or	black pepper
halibut fillets	¼ cup cracker crumbs

Preheat oven to 350° F. Sauté shallots in butter, but do not allow to blacken or overcook. Place fish in a shallow casserole; top with shallots, then heavy cream. Add clams and half the liquid from the can (sauce should not be watery). Sprinkle with salt and pepper and top with buttered crumbs. Bake about 30 minutes.

If you wish, brown crumbs under broiler a few seconds before serving. Serve at once. Rice or boiled potatoes are a good accompaniment.

As I set down these next recipes, I feel a little sentimental. Not about the food, which is scrumptious. Prepare it and eat it and be forever glad. My sentimentality has to do with the lady who gave me the recipes. Mrs. Carl Holmes, blue-eyed Bubbles.

She has always been called Bubbles by everyone, but she was christened Nancy Ryan and she was English-born and English-bred. Our days in the theatre coincided and occasionally we appeared together in the same play. That was the era of the drawing-room comedy and although I don't suppose they would stand up today—it has been years since I read one—in their time they had a good deal to recommend them. They were literate and witty and elegant. And knowing that I am hopelessly dated when I say it, I still prefer them to *Hair* or *Jesus Christ Superstar* or *Lenny,* although the last was redeemed by the electrifying performance of Cliff Gorman in the title role.

English actors used to be considered better bred than Americans. I do not vouch for the truth or falsehood of the opinion, but for the most part they certainly spoke better English. At least it was more English English and went down well in plays by Mr. Frederick Lonsdale and Mr. Somerset Maugham who *were* British and slipped easily enough into plays by Mr. Philip Barry and Mr. Sam Behrman, members of the American team.

Being English, Bubbles was sought after to play light comedy parts in light comedies. I was not English but I had been educated or, more accurately, I had passed through assorted finishing schools and I had attended school in France. I was considered a "lady" type. Bitchy, as a rule, but a lady. Was I ever entranced when I had an opportunity to play light comedy non-bitches! But what an actress senses she is capable of and what producers and directors are convinced she can and cannot do, do not necessarily coincide.

In any event, in the days when Bubbles and I were co-operating in bringing to the public the lighthearted messages of urbane playwrights, Washington was a great tryout town. Many plays opened there, usually having been broken in by four previous performances: Thursday, Friday and the two Saturday shows in Wilmington, Delaware.

The diplomatic corps and the actresses were congenial and the high jinks entertaining. Some of the ambassadorial shenanigans were sweet and memorable and all were amusing.

Not long ago Bubbles and Carl came to dine with us in the country. Bubbles and I were reminiscing about the innocent pleasures of our youth, when our husbands came out on the terrace and it seemed wiser to switch our conversation to shoes and ships and sealing wax.

When I mentioned this book, Mr. and Mrs. Holmes, who are keenly aware that good eating is a virtue and a grace, volunteered to go into conference with their staff, which is of impressive proportions and highly skilled and send along a few contributions.

The following is a suggested menu for an elegant luncheon. Recipes follow for the two starred items.

Eggs in Eggs*
Cold Duck à l'Orange
Melon Dessert*

Eggs in Eggs
(Serves 6)

| 6 eggs | Bread crumbs |
| Flour | Deep fat |

Place six eggs at room temperature into boiling water and boil for nine minutes.

Pour off water, fill pot immediately with cold water to stop the cooking process, and let the eggs cool in the water.

When cool, cut the eggs in half. Dust lightly with a little seasoned flour. Dip into a couple of beaten eggs, roll in bread crumbs and fry in deep fat. Serve with Hollandaise sauce.

Melon Dessert

Small cantaloupe	Vanilla ice cream or lemon ice
Cointreau	Freshly grated coconut
Maple syrup	Fresh mint

Cut the cantaloupe in half. Remove seeds. Pour in a small amount of Cointreau and a little bit of maple syrup. Refrigerate until well chilled. When ready to serve, place a scoop of vanilla ice cream or lemon ice in the cantaloupe, sprinkle with freshly grated coconut, and top with a sprig of fresh mint.

Two other mouth-watering specialties of the house of Holmes are chicken bourguignon and a hot lemon soufflé.

The bird first. This one is not simple. It's merely great. To be sure, it's so gussied up you may not realize you're eating chicken, but it's instructive to learn how the other half lives.

Chicken Bourguignon

(Serves 6)

6 chicken breasts, skinned and boned	2 teaspoons chopped garlic
	2 tablespoons chopped shallots
Lemon juice	2 tablespoons chopped fresh
Salt and pepper	tarragon or 3 tablespoons
Brandy	dried tarragon
¼ pound Swiss cheese, grated	2 tablespoons flour or cornstarch
¼ pound boiled ham, finely chopped	1 tablespoon meat glaze
	1¼ cups chicken broth
¼ pound mushrooms, finely chopped	¼ cup sherry
	1 cup dry red wine
1 black truffle, finely chopped	Salt and pepper to taste
4 tablespoons butter	2 teaspoons guava jelly
2 tablespoons brandy, warmed	

Rinse chicken breasts in lemon juice; dry on paper towels.

With a sharp knife, slit a pocket in each breast. Season with salt and pepper, brush with brandy. Combine the grated cheese, boiled ham, mushrooms, and truffle. Stuff each pocket with some of the mixture.

In a large pan, heat butter till foamy; add the chicken. Cover with flat lid—what is called a bacon press, usually made of Pyrex is good—and place a weight on top. Brown the breasts on one side, turn, and brown on other side. Flame with the 2 tablespoons brandy. Remove chicken, set aside, and keep warm.

In same pan, add the garlic and shallots and sauté about 2 minutes. Remove pan from heat; add remaining ingredients except guava jelly. Place on heat, and when mixture comes to a boil, add jelly. Add chicken to pan, cook slowly for about 20 minutes. Check seasoning and serve.

Hot Lemon Soufflé with Sauce

(Serves 6–8)

4 tablespoons sweet butter	¼ cup lemon juice
4 tablespoons flour	4 tablespoons confectioners'
Pinch of salt	sugar
1½ cups milk	6 egg yolks
2 tablespoons grated lemon	8 egg whites
rind	

Preheat oven to 375° F. Prepare a 2-quart soufflé dish as follows: tie a collar of wax paper around soufflé dish so that it extends 2 to 3 inches above edge of dish. Grease dish and paper with butter; sprinkle with granulated sugar; set aside.

In saucepan, melt butter; blend in flour, salt, and then milk. Cook over medium heat, stirring constantly until thickened. Remove from heat; add lemon rind and lemon juice. Blend in the confectioners' sugar, and the egg yolks one at a time, beating after each addition.

Place egg whites in mixing bowl; beat until stiff but not dry. Fold into the lemon mixture. Pour into prepared soufflé dish; sprinkle top with some confectioners' sugar. Set in pan of boiling water; bake 50 minutes.

Lemon Sauce for Soufflé

1 egg	1 tablespoon grated lemon rind
2 egg yolks	2 tablespoons kirsch
3 tablespoons lemon juice	¼ cup granulated sugar
Pinch of salt	

Combine all ingredients in a bowl. Set the bowl in a pan of hot water over heat. Beat with wire whisk until thick. Remove from heat and remove bowl from pan of water. Cover with Saran Wrap so crust will not form on top. Serve with the lemon soufflé.

The Holmes recipes are delicious, but there is no question that they are elaborate. And I've even simplified them a bit!

A somewhat different approach is followed by my stepson Peter Brown. Peter likes to eat, but he doesn't want to spend his days in preparation.

The year he passed a summer in St. Tropez he came back with the following trophy. There are fancier ways of doing a ratatouille, but this is quick and very good. It goes well with almost any kind of meat and may be served hot or cold.

Ratatouille

(Serves 4–6)

1 large onion, chopped	2 or 3 tomatoes, peeled and
2 cloves garlic, chopped	quartered
4 tablespoons olive oil	1 green pepper, cut into
2 small eggplant, peeled and	julienne strips
sliced	Salt and pepper to taste
3 or 4 zucchini, sliced	

Sauté onion and garlic in 2 tablespoons of the olive oil until tender. Add remaining ingredients; add the remaining olive oil (might need more). Cover tightly and simmer over low heat about 45 minutes.

This next recipe comes from France too. This time from Paris and Mrs. Geoffrey Parsons

Veal Kidneys Flambé
(Serves 4)

4 veal kidneys	1 tablespoon pâté de foie gras *or*
⅓ cup butter	4 chicken livers, sautéed and
½ cup (4 ounces) brandy	mashed
⅛ teaspoon dry mustard *or*	Salt and pepper
1 teaspoon Dijon-style mustard	¼ cup heavy cream
1 tablespoon lemon juice	

Have the butcher remove the fat from the veal kidneys and leave them whole. Wash in cold water. Skin and remove any left-over bits of fat. In skillet, melt butter; when foaming, add kidneys and sauté for about 5 minutes over medium heat.

Warm brandy, pour over kidneys, and light. When flame has died down, remove kidneys and keep warm. Allow liquid in pan to simmer and reduce for 5 minutes. Add the mustard and lemon juice. Should you have any pâté de foie gras add it to the sauce. Otherwise, the chicken livers are a nice touch. Add kidneys, salt, pepper, and heavy cream. Heat, but don't allow cream to boil. Serve with rice.

As a green vegetable accompaniment Mrs. Parsons suggests purée of string beans.

Purée of String Beans

String beans
Lemon juice
Sour cream

Undercook beans in a little rapidly boiling salted water. Drain, and put through a food mill. Sprinkle with a teaspoon of lemon juice and add a dollop of sour cream.

Two of our oldest friends are Drue and Geoffrey Parsons, who have a delightful flat on the Île Saint Louis in Paris and an impressive house in Spain.

Whenever Norton and I are in Europe we visit them and we eat very well indeed, the earth and its fruits being a passion of Madame's.

Drue is what I call a true cook—basic, one might say. She was in the French Resistance movement during the war, and alone on her farm near Paris, where she sheltered Allied airmen who had been shot down by the Germans, she killed her own chickens and rabbits.

However, before her days of courage and grandeur she too worked in the theatre. One summer she was playing at Dennis on Cape Cod. I was out of a job, so I went to spend a few weeks with her.

In such time as was left between rehearsals and performances we enjoyed ourselves and embraced nature; the sea, the fields, and little birds. A nest of baby robins tumbled from a tree, their parents defected, and Drue and I adopted them. We fed them hamburger. Hamburger was protein and looked like worms. Not to baby robins. We woke one morning to three little featherless corpses. After that we left nature to her own devices.

Since Drue was in the theatre most of the day the housekeeping devolved upon me. We lived in a matchbox, so it wasn't too arduous. I have time, I thought, why not apply myself to cooking? There was a two-burner kerosene stove with a vague sort of oven attachment and Drue had a cookbook full of tempting recipes.

I went to work with a will. Even had she been famous then, Julia Child would not have felt that she had met her match, but I was pretty pleased with my results and Drue, loyal friend and hungry actress that she was, courteously devoured them.

We had a couple of beaux at the time and once when they came to see us I fed them. After that they always suggested eating out, but they were relatively well heeled—compared to the poor actors they were a pair of Croesuses—and we put their offer down to good manners and generosity.

174

One day I said to Drue, "You know, Crisco is absolutely *marvelous*—it goes with *everything*. How have I ever managed without it all my life?"

My friend looked at me thoughtfully. "Dear," she said, "that book you're using, it's put out by the Crisco people."

Today I make no pretensions to being an expert cook. I am not but I know more than I did and I know that good food and good wine rank high among the blessings of civilization. That particular book and the kerosene burners are behind me. Be of good cheer. If I can come a long way, so can you.

O33